Building a Healthier Whole You After a Divorce or Unhealthy Relationship

Renita Adira

Copyright © 2020 by Renita Adira

All Rights Reserved

BUILDING A HEALTHIER WHOLE YOU

AFTER A DIVORCE OR UNHEALTHY RELATIONSHIP

by Renita Adira

Published by PREMIUM PUBLICATIONS

PO Box 891

Crown Point, IN. 46308

www.premiumpublications.org

Printed in the United States of America

This workbook or parts thereof may not be used or reproduced in any form, stored in a retrieval system, or transmitted in any form by any means electronic, mechanical, photocopy, recording or otherwise without prior written permission of the publisher, except as provided by United States of America copyright law.

First Edition
Cover Design/Layout by Obinna Ozuo

Library of Congress Control Number: 2020916303

ISBN: 978-0-9977451-1-5

This workbook is dedicated to anyone

Who has gone through the after math of starting over after an unsuccessful Marriage or Relationship.

Also, to the many people who struggle with the shame of being divorce multiple times and starting over.

My desire is to encourage people all over the world who struggle with starting over again.

I dedicate this workbook with hopes that it will bring healing and the strength to start over.

Introduction

Here is what this workbook is going to help you to do, it's going to teach you how to start over after leaving an unhealthy marriage or relationship. It's going to give you the strength, encouragement and empowerment to live again while picking up the broken pieces. It will also help you to work through being bitter, angry, hurt, broken or feeling a sense of shame from being in a dysfunctional or unhealthy relationship or marriage.

This workbook will give you the confidence and reassurance that is needed to start over so that you can become a healthier and whole person again. This workbook is designed to take you from blaming to doing the necessary work that is needed so that you can heal with the proper self-trust, self-esteem and self-assurance needed to explore the greatness that lives inside of you. It will teach you how to be restored while you are learning, growing, healing and being rebuilt into a better version of you.

It will also teach you how to take one day at a time and one step at a time. This workbook will teach you to identify the red flags and the toxicity of being in an unhealthy relationship or marriage. This workbook will assist with helping you to work through your own personal imperfections and flaws as you work the process. By the end of this workbook you will have experienced a healthier way of starting over after a divorce or unhealthy relationship.

Life after a Divorce and Starting Over

Contents

    Introduction 4
1. Timing 7
2. Who Am I 13
3. How Do I start Over? 19
4. What did I lose 25
5. What did I Gain 31
6. Every man is not like the last one 37
7. Every woman is not like the last one 45
8. What Should Or Shouldn't Matter 53
9. Let Go 61
10. No Contact 69
11. How do I Love Me Again? 79
12. Picking Up the Piece's 87
13. The Stigma Behind Divorce 95
14. Learning To Identify Your Strength And Weaknesses 103
15. How To Move Forward Without Feeling A Sense Of Shame 111
16. Caring For You In A Healthy Manner 119
17. What To Do When Bitterness And Anger Set In 127
18. Living A Life Filled With Peace And Joy 135
19. How Do I Enjoy Life Being Single? 143
20. How To Press Through Life Even When You Are Hurting 151
21. How To Get Back Up Once You Have Fallen 159
22. The Power Of One 167
23. Hope Deferred 175
24. How to live a purposeful life after the divorce or the relationship has ended? .. 185

Timing

There is a time for everything. Sometimes people can rush into another relationship or marriage with the thought that I am healed or with the mindset that says, I haven't been affected by the things that happened in the last marriage or relationship. This can sometimes lead to premature relationships or marriages. Rather there is denial or broken focus there should be time between the last relationship or marriage that you were in.

It is important that you allow the proper time to heal before you enter into the next marriage or relationship, so that you can evaluate what worked and what didn't work. Also, what could have been done differently or better before you enter into another relationship or marriage. I am not saying that you should beat yourself up about every single thing that happened, but you do need to be honest and examine your faults and flaws as well. When you are able to admit your faults then you are able to build on your strengths.

When you are in a relationship or marriage no matter how much you like to believe that you were the perfect person in that relationship or marriage; I am here to tell you that you too played a part in some of the disagreements, even if it was a little part you still had a part. The reason why I am able to say this is because there isn't one person to blame when it comes to who is right or wrong. There is always a 1% of uncertainty or fault and on top of that it says that you are perfect and no human being is perfect; we all come with our own set of flaws and blemishes. Before you enter into another marriage or relationship ask yourself the key questions.

Key Questions to Ask:

- Have I done the work that's needed before entering into a new relationship or marriage?

  _____
  _____
  _____

- Is this the right time for me to enter into a marriage or relationship?

  _____
  _____
  _____

- Am I being honest with myself?

  _____
  _____
  _____

- Am I being with someone because I am trying to get over the last person who I was with?

  _____
  _____
  _____

- Am I blaming myself for the things that happened in the marriage or relationship?

  _____
  _____
  _____

- Do I carry shame and embarrassment from the last relationship or unsuccessful marriage/s?

  _____
  _____
  _____

- Am I willing and ready to do the necessary work so that my next relationship or marriage can be healthier and balanced?

  _____
  _____
  _____

- Have I gotten over the things that happened in my last relationship or marriage?

  _____
  _____
  _____

- Have I forgiven myself and the other person?

  _____
  _____
  _____

- Am I mentally ready to be in another relationship or marriage?

  _____
  _____
  _____

- Have I dealt with any serious issues that may have required counseling?

  _____
  _____
  _____

- How much time has gone pass since my last relationship or marriage?
  _____
  _____
  _____

- Am I entering into another relationship or marriage because I am lonely?
  _____
  _____
  _____

- Is my heart cleansed of any and all hatred, bitterness, fear, hurt or anger?
  _____
  _____
  _____

Now you add some of your own questions or thoughts

Key Factors to Remember:

- If you don't see about you then who will
- Your healing process will take time
- You are at your best and able to give your best when you have been restored to a healthy place mentally, emotionally, physically and for some spiritually
- If you don't give yourself the proper time after each relationship or marriage, then you should expect to keep getting the same results if not worse
- Premature relationships or marriages can do more harm than good
- No one is perfect but timing allows for the proper evaluation of things
- People make mistakes and sometimes things happen that are out of our control
- Some say time heals all wounds but I say that self-care along with time shapes and cultivates the proper healing
- Don't be anxious for another relationship or marriage before properly healing
- Grow, Mature, Believe, and work towards a healthier you
- Don't store up years of pain and hurt take the time to do some soul searching and allow healing from within and it will manifest on the outside

Who Am I

Oftentimes when coming out of a marriage or relationship you lose sight of who you are as a person and an individual. The reason for this is, many of you have given a substantial amount of yourself rather it was your time, years, money, love, dedication and so much more to the marriage or relationship to only come to the realization that you have wasted more than you have gained. That's not uncommon after coming out of an unsuccessful relationship or marriage. You began to have all of these different feelings, thoughts and emotions that seems as though they hit you all at once.

It can feel like a ton of bricks that have fallen down on you. It can also feel as though something has sucked the very breath out of you which can make you feel as though you are grasping for air. There are so many broken pieces to pick up when coming out of an unsuccessful marriage or relationship, it literally can leave you in a place where you don't know who you are. Depending on how long you were in the marriage or relationship and how much you have given to the building of that marriage or relationship the repair process of who you are as an individual can be a long and lengthy process.

This doesn't mean that it can't be done it just means be prepared to do some self-work. This is not a time where you beat yourself up about everything that didn't work out or why it didn't work out, but this is really a time where you take the time to seek out who you are again as a person who is no longer connected to someone else. If you use this time now that you are single to ponder on all of the bad things or the what if's; you will do yourself a disservice in your own personal healing in restoring who you are now that you are single. After you have gotten over being angry and bitter, and the pain and hurt of it all; and you have truly allowed yourself to grieve; this process of seeking Who Am I, will allow you to begin to open the door to seek true healing.

This process isn't about the other person or what you gave to the other person or the marriage or relationship, this process is truly about the rebuilding of you. This process also will allow you to say, I was lost but now I am found. Who Am I, jumpstarts the process of allowing you to live again. In this process you will give yourself the permission without any condemnation to be free to be you without the shame that many people attach to divorce or unsuccessful relationships.

Key Questions to Ask:

- Who are you now that you are single and without a partner?

  _____
  _____
  _____

- Are you putting in the necessary self-work?

  _____
  _____
  _____

- Have you made Who Am I about you and not the other person?

  _____
  _____
  _____

- Have you given yourself permission and validated yourself to live again, if not why?

  _____
  _____
  _____

- Have you come to the place where the divorce or relationship no longer defines who you are as a person?

  _____
  _____
  _____

- What is one thing that you have learned about who you are?

  _____
  _____
  _____

- What are your expectation for you now that you are single?

  _____
  _____
  _____

- Do you find it to be challenging learning who you are again?

  _____
  _____
  _____

Now you add some of your own questions or thoughts

Key Factors to Remember:

- Picking up the pieces is about you and only you

- Never stop believing in you no matter how old you are

- Restoration and healing starts with you

- True happiness is within not what comes from another person

- You still have good years in you no matter what you gave out

- Everyday that you have breath inhale and exhale at the pace that flows for you

- This too shall pass

- Don't continue to blame or burden yourself

- Don't stop loving you even when others have

- Always be your number one cheerleader even when no one is cheering

- The marriage or relationship ended don't you end with it

- Allow the old person to die but birth and bring forth the new person which has been hidden

- Define who you are in your singleness

- What has broken you allow it to rebirth you

- Never give up on you even when others have

- Say I am Worthy, I am Valuable, I am not what I have been through

- Remember to keep pressing, press like you never have because this one is for you

How Do I start Over?

Starting over is never easy, but we all have to start somewhere. Starting over can be scary and can come with many fears and uncertainties. Starting over can come with anxiety, depression, loneliness, sadness and so much more. That's not to say that you can't or you won't get through it, what it says is that you have to want it for yourself while all the guilt, hurt, pain and shame is showing up at the same time. When these things all show up at the same time it can make starting over more difficult. Starting over is not impossible it just takes a little time and work. The biggest question that many people have is how do I start over?

One day at a time, One step at a time and One breath at a time. Allow the process to take place and don't rush it but embrace it so that you can allow yourself the proper time to grieve, breath, grow, mature, heal and be restored to your whole self. Starting over isn't always bad. Starting over can and will allow you a new blueprint to life and a opportunity to build or restructure a sturdy foundation that will lead to a stronger and better you.

Everything in life comes with an associated cost rather good or bad or happy or sad. If you live long enough life will show you so many sides of it; as will people. Some of the daily challenges and many difficulties that one may face in life will literally make your head spin. Most things in life doesn't come easy but making the decision to start will most definitely be worth it as it pertains to you. Don't allow your perception of a thing to be so far off to where you don't allow yourself a start over moment; after all you owe it to yourself. Starting over isn't about how you look after the unsuccessful marriage or relationship, it is about how you bounce back and what did you learn from it.

Don't allow life failures to destroy you but use each lesson as a learning tool to make you a better you. Starting over isn't always pleasant but you have to believe that you are worth it. Starting over can come with its own set of barriers but not starting at all can also come with its challenges. Make the decision to start and remember quitting isn't an option. Take your time, get your momentum and once you gain enough momentum and strength take off and don't allow nothing and nobody to hold you down not even yourself.

Key Questions to Ask:

- Are you ready to start over and if not why?

  _____
  _____
  _____

- Are you still too angry or hurt to start over?

  _____
  _____
  _____

- Have you given thought as to when you want to start the process to start over?

  _____
  _____
  _____

- Do you know how to start over?

  _____
  _____
  _____

- Have you allowed yourself the proper time to grieve?

  _____
  _____
  _____

- Do you know that there will never be a magical or perfect time to start over you have to make the choice and decision to start over?

  _____
  _____
  _____

- Do you know that starting over starts with you?

_____

_____

_____

Now you add some of your own questions or thoughts

Key Factors to Remember:

- Starting over isn't always easy but you are worth it
- Remember you have to take the initiative to start somewhere
- You have to challenge yourself even when it hurts for the betterment of you
- Remember you are being stretched but it's worth it because it's for you
- There is no comfort in pain or sacrifice
- Remember don't give up on you, say, I am not a quitter
- Remember to love you regardless of the struggle or the difficult moments in life that you face
- Remember starting over is for you and about you and not the other person
- What you gain is, your life back, self-worth, dignity, respect, peace, joy, happiness and a better healthier you
- Remember starting over is worth it because you are worth it
- Believe in you even when it seems hard
- Remember to say, I am going to endure the process of starting over so that I can live again
- Everything that ends doesn't always have to bring bad results
- My mind is the training ground for new growth and development
- I am never too old to have a fresh start
- All is not lost in a fresh start especially when the start is for me

What did I lose

You can write a laundry list of things that were lost, some of which you can get back and some in which you will never be able to get back. That's not to downplay the losses but that's not to keep the focus on the losses either. Being in a marriage or relationship is going to come with its own set of losses, especially when exiting. I wish that I can say all these great things but the fact of the matter is that a loss is just what it is a loss, there is no easy way around that.

However, your perception about the loss can change or reshape the lost. What I mean by that is, if you lost someone who was selfish, uncaring, abusive, manipulative, cheap or someone who committed adultery or someone who was a liar or a cheater; What did you really loose? Yeah you can say you lost your time, money, years, and pieces of you, and the list can go on.

But now that you have been granted the opportunity to be set free from all the things that wasn't making the marriage or relationship work for whatever reasons, how was that a lost? Follow me, it's the familiarity of what you were in, the union of two, the small things that, that person did, and the fact that you could say that you had someone verses now you don't. Also the times when things were good or ok which gave you momentary happiness; or the fact that no matter how rotten to the core the person was you were able to say we been together for this many years.

However, you look at it, was it really a win? Maybe small wins but not enough to keep the marriage or relationship pieced together. The tools and resources and willingness to change, grow and build wasn't strong enough any longer to hold all the broken pieces together. The glue and tape stop holding the pieces together because things had gotten so enormous without the proper care and the willingness to change to the point it had no other choice but to dissolve. Sometimes people get so caught up in the drama and trauma of the dysfunction of the relationship or marriage until they have allowed it to be their new normal.

They have either turned the blind eye to hold on to what they believed to be functional or just outright ignored the dysfunction to the point they have lost sight of reality. Either way you look at it they have lost and been losing for some time. Some people check out of a relationship or marriage way before it actually ends where they actually walk away from one another.

Most people stay hoping that things will get better but many have become immune to the trauma and drama while other people have just allowed themselves to become so lost in the marriage or relationship they fear to leave. Don't look at all that you have lost but look at what you can regain if you give yourself the opportunity to do so. Don't dwell on the losses but focus on what those life lessons and dysfunctions have taught you.

Key Questions to Ask:

- How am I viewing my losses?

  _____
  _____
  _____

- How do I turn my losses into wins?

  _____
  _____
  _____

- What is my true perception about the losses?

  _____
  _____
  _____

- Am I harboring too much on the losses to the point where I am not allowing my healing to come forth?

  _____
  _____
  _____

- Am I allowing the losses to take up space in my mind that is affecting my growth and or healing?

  _____
  _____
  _____

- Do you believe that you owe yourself a second chance at life rather you have a partner or not?

  _____
  _____
  _____

- Do you believe that you can do life by yourself if you just had to?

  _____
  _____
  _____

Now you add some of your own questions or thoughts

Key Factors to Remember:

- You didn't lose anyone that was healthy for you, if they left or you had to make the choice to leave them, be thankful for your new beginning

- Remember you owe yourself the opportunity to live life rather by yourself or with a partner

- Remember life is what you make it

- I am more than my losses

- I won't allow my losses to shape who I am as a person or have the last word as to how my life is suppose to be

- Losses can be wins but I have to allow myself to view the losses differently

- I am an important creation, I am unique and there is none other like me

- I am a powerhouse all by myself

- I am a leader who won't allow life challenges to rob me of my purpose or destiny

- Losses don't define me as a person

- I will allow the losses to build me and not break me

- I will allow the losses, the brokenness, the tears and the sacrifices to rebuild me back into a whole person

- My gifts, my greatness and all that is within me will deliver me and push me to higher heights

- I will view my losses as wins and from this day forth everything is a win, win for me

What did I Gain

Some would say I've gained nothing, I have lost everything and I have even lost myself. Other's would say that I've gained nothing worth talking about. Many would say I wasted my best years, I've gained nothing but humiliation, shame, defeat and I was made a fool of and I have experienced great sorrow and more. The answer will vary depending on who you ask. This is true in many cases. But when you look at the question under a different set of lenses and not from a place of pain and hurt you will be able to answer this question a little differently.

Example, if you really set down with your thoughts not your pain you will be able to extrapolate the many gains and not cast all your cares and focus on the losses or pain. Let's take a look at some gains when the mind isn't sitting with the pain. One you are in a better place mentally, physically, emotionally and for some spiritually. Two, you have more peace and joy in your life. Three, you are no longer being traumatized by all the unnecessary drama and abuse. Four you are now able to think and make decisions from a healthier place and not a broken place or a place of confusion.

You are now given the opportunity to be a whole person and your best person without all the anxiety and what if's. You are not being mentally abused, physically, or emotionally abused or tormented in your spirit where you feel like you are on the edge all the time. Your mind isn't being left to figure out what your partner is doing when he or she fails to effectively communicate to you and the list goes on. The Gain is that you get to rebuild on a fresh start of serenity, tranquility, and retreat to a place more productive and conducive for you. So if you really look at what you have gained, you have gained more than you lost not looking at material or monetary things but from the whole person analogy of your losses and your gains.

I am a firm believe that when life knocks you down get back up. There will be storms, testes and challenges that will come to test the very being of your person. Some we have placed ourselves in and others we never asked for or even thought of. Nevertheless, don't lose sight of what you have gained. Everything bad isn't always bad just like everything good isn't always good. There are pros and cons to everything in life, you just have to be open and willing to calibrate your scale when it is off balance.

Key Questions to Ask:

- Do you keep pressing replay on all the losses and giving no attention to your gains?

- Do you believe that you are a good person in spite of what you have been through?

- Do you believe or feed off of all the bad things that you have told yourself or your ex-partner has said to you?

- Do you want to be free from the bad and traumatizing experiences?

- Do you believe that true change starts and ends with you?

- Can you identify your Gains?

  _____
  _____
  _____

- What is a Gain to you?

  _____
  _____
  _____

- Are you willing and ready to add to your Gains?

  _____
  _____
  _____

Now you add some of your own questions or thoughts

Key Factors to Remember:

- Remember Everyone Gain will look different
- Remember everyone process will look different
- No two situations are the same they may appear similar but different in its own way
- Don't get so caught up on the losses that you can't add to your gains
- Remember that no one asks for bad things to happen they just do and sometimes to good people
- Don't allow the storms to change you, grow and reinvent or invent who you are
- Nobody can do the work of self-healing for you but you
- Don't be so hard on yourself to the point that you lose focus on the needed work that needs to take place in your own personal life
- Self-reflect but don't self-damage
- Allow the bad to be turned around and work for your good
- G- Gratuity
- A- Awakening
- I- Individuality
- N- New Life
- Gain your own trust back and don't beat yourself up
- Learn to love you if you don't already and if you do fall deeper in love with you, not in a vain way but in a healthy way that elevates your thought process to allow healing and growth

Every man is not like the last one

There are many reasons why people no longer work together as a couple, the list can go on and on. However, whatever your reason was that you and your ex or significant other stop working; I want you to remember that ever man or all men are not like the last one. If you view all men like the last one, then you will view men to be painful and hurtful beings no matter the age or the man. I say that to say when you are able to let go of the pain, hurt, bitterness, grief, anger, and painful memories then and only then will you allow yourself to live again.

Having a belief that every man isn't like the last one will also allow you to be open to date or even marry another man without the preconception that they are all alike. But just like anything else you have to get rid of the toxic waste and pain from the previous marriage or relationship along with the old mindset that was traumatized. If you continue to carry those thoughts with you, I guarantee that you will bring all of the old luggage from that old marriage or relationship into your new. Once that happens the relationship or marriage is dome to fail.

Nevertheless, the key point of it all is rather you decide to enter into another marriage or relationship you still have to give or allow yourself the opportunity to heal and not view men in a negative light because of your past experiences. Just because the last man caused unnecessary trauma wounds doesn't mean that will be the experience of all men. There are still some good men in the world. The only way that you can take your life back is to put in the necessary work that it will take to be healed. That doesn't come with beating yourself up for the many years that you gave of yourself in the last marriage or relationship. Your healing and or restoration should look differently than the pain that you endured. The other part that goes along with your healing that you should keep in mind; is all men didn't hurt you, it was the last man.

This wasn't an encounter with all men, just the one. And if there were other men that has caused you great pain then you really need to take the time to allow yourself to grieve and do some self-work, because what that is possibly saying is that you have somethings that are broken within self and you need to identify what it is or what they are before you enter into another relationship or marriage.

Key Questions to Ask:

- Are you angry at all men or just the one and if so why won't you let it go?

_____

_____

_____

- Are you continually replaying all the negative things that happened or things that was said in your mind and if so why?

_____

_____

_____

- How long will you allow yourself to hold on to the pain before you allow yourself to be healed?

_____

_____

_____

- Do you believe that you can pick up or create a life outside of what you had with your ex?

_____

_____

_____

- Are you fearful to live life now that you are no longer with your ex?

_____

_____

_____

- Do you believe that you are worth a second chance even if your second chance is you being alone?

  _____
  _____
  _____

- Do you believe in yourself? If the answer is no, will you allow yourself to start to believe in you?

  _____
  _____
  _____

Now you add some of your own questions or thoughts

Key Factors to Remember:

- Every man won't be like the last one but every man does come with their own set of imperfections and or flaws

- Always remember nothing or no one is perfect including myself

- Anything that you want to work you have to keep the maintenance up on it, meaning always equipping yourself and your partner with new tools and resources that aid in the continual growth of the marriage or the relationship

- Marriage requires constant work not part-time work

- No two men are alike

- Sometimes the fall isn't always meant to destroy you, but it can be used to build you

- Falls oftentimes can test or show you what you have or had in that particular marriage or relationship

- As long as you keep living you will endure certain test in life and not all of them will be bad and not all of them will feel good but the end result can be good if you learn from the mistakes

- People change along the way and sometimes for the good and sometimes for the bad

- Don't allow the last man to change the beauty that lives on the inside of you

- Don't allow the situation to change who you are or turn you into someone that you are not

- If you chose to date or get married again that is a personal choice but heal yourself first

- Don't be anxious but take one day at a time and one step at a time
- Be free to be you and fall in love with yourself again; nurture your wounds back to health

Every woman is not like the last one

Don't make the mistake of thinking that every woman is like the last one because of your past experience. You shouldn't allow your past experience that you had with the last woman to be the same experience with a new woman. You also shouldn't think that all women are like the last one. There are no two people who are completely alike. If you allow yourself to think that every woman is just like the last one, you will kill the new relationship or marriage before you allow it to grow any good root, if not badly damage it.

If you keep your old mindset and you hold your guard up so high about the things that the last woman has done, or the things that may resemble what you went through in the last relationship; that may show up in your new marriage or relationship it will cause for you to react in a negative manner. Once you have taken the time to heal, grow, mature, and learn from the last relationship or marriage you should be able to talk about issues that arise that may be the same or look the same but slightly different and come out with a healthier outcome.

If you don't give the new person a chance to grow from her mistakes and fix her wrongs while with you without any pre-judgements or convictions, then what that shows is maybe you still have work to do within self. It can also show that you could be possibly still operating from an old and sick mindset. If that is the case this may cause for you to be quick to judge the new person harshly because of the mistakes of the last woman. What later ends up happening is, you will learn that you haven't given the new woman any room to make her own mistakes regardless if they resemble some of the same ones from a previous marriage or relationship. Assuming that the mistakes or issues aren't major or total deal breakers for being in a healthy marriage or relationship.

After your healing process has taken place and you have decided to start a new relationship or marriage you should be at a place where you have learned to work through some of the things that once was an issue for you if the new person so happens to show that same problem; again assuming that it is a durable and workable problem. Some women learn faster than other women and the new woman may be willing to correct her wrongs quicker than the last woman was willing to do.

Nevertheless, when you have already found her to be guilty without allowing her the opportunity to fix any of her mistakes so that she can learn and grow from her mistakes; then you become the guilty one, not her. Some women may come with some of the same mistakes, flaws, or imperfections as the last woman or you might see some small resemblance. However, if you give the new woman the benefit of the doubt that her willingness to change may be different from the last woman then you can say that you have given the opportunity for change.

Now on the flip side of that, there may be some signs that will present themselves as red flags. I am not saying don't pay attention to the signs; but when and if they shall happen to appear, have an open and clear mind that she isn't like the last woman. What I am saying is allow her to show you a different outcome without condemning her first. There are still some good women in the world, don't count them all out.

Allow your new partner the chance to show her goodness and give her the opportunity to show the fruit that she possess. Starting over starts with you first, you can't take old and weighted luggage and an old mindset into something new and expect it to be healthy. Take the time to heal your mind and heart. Give your mind a renewed mindset and your heart a good cleanse and allow the wounds from the last marriage or relationship to be repaired and healed.

Key Questions to Ask:

- Have I done the necessary work that needed to be done for myself?

- Am I ready to start dating or to be in another marriage?

- Am I healed of all past wounds?

- Have I renewed my mindset to be in a healthier marriage or relationship?

- Do I have my guards up so high that I am too guarded?

- Do I still have open wounds?

- Are my scars so bad that I am not willing to put in the work for me to be healed?

  _____
  _____
  _____

- Have I cleansed my heart of all the pain that took up residence?

  _____
  _____
  _____

- Have I stopped pressing the rewind button on all the faults of the last woman and all that she did or didn't do?

  _____
  _____
  _____

- Am I moving too fast to be with someone because I am lonely?

  _____
  _____
  _____

- Do I feel that forming a sexual bond with another woman before healing will heal my wounds or help me to get over the last woman?

  _____
  _____
  _____

Now you add some of your own questions or thoughts

Key Factors to Remember:

- What good is it to enter into another marriage or relationship if you don't do the self-care that is needed, because you will only end up with the same problems if not worst

- A woman was created to be your help mate and you should love and care for her as such

- Don't allow the last woman to change you in a negative way

- Remember that every woman isn't like the last one

- Remember that if you are still broken you will bring that brokenness into your new marriage or relationship

- Don't be afraid to give of yourself to the right woman, you will know her if you take the time to learn her, dwell with her and study her

- Don't allow the heartache of one woman to stop you from loving again

- Remember love doesn't hurt, that person hurt you

- Remember to buy books or listen to teachings that can give you the tools that you lack

- Not everyone is going to be born knowing everything, if you seek you shall find in more ways than one

- Don't make excuses put in the time and work to make you your best person, no one can do that but you

- Don't allow what you didn't get in life to hold you back from being who you were created to be, forgive and move on

What Should Or Shouldn't Matter

What should matter is that you are a healthier person and that you have been made whole and restored from your last relationship or marriage. What's most important is that you have allowed yourself the proper time to heal and you have learned from the mistakes that were made. If you can say that you have done the work physically, emotionally, mentally, and for some spiritually and you have dealt with the damage that was done to you and you are no longer focusing on the other person and you have a clear mind and you don't hold any faults or un-forgiveness in your heart then that is what matters.

What also should matter is when you wake up and you no longer are thinking about the other person and the things that went wrong in the previous marriage or relationship. Some people leave relationships or a marriage and are so badly damaged to the point where they don't come back from the pain or hurt. What matters is that you have done the work in the areas that are needed so that you are your best person; first for you and second for anyone else that you chose to be with. It doesn't matter who thinks you are ready for a relationship or a marriage; you have to know for yourself when you are ready.

Don't continue to live in a place of pain or hurt. It's ok to take the necessary time to grieve but don't get stuck in the grievance process. What should matter is that you are not being asked to rush your process to a time frame that fits the need of someone else rather than your own. What should matter is that you are focused and not looking at other's who are in a relationship or marriage and you rush your process of healing to have someone. Also, it shouldn't matter that you are tired of doing things alone or that you feel lonely because you don't have a partner. It shouldn't matter that people are or have approached you to want to get to know you if you haven't completed your healing process. If you pay attention to all the things that don't matter verses what really matters you will never complete your process in a healthy manner.

You will leave yourself open for many excuses and all reasons as to why you didn't work your process of healing for yourself or why you half way completed it. People are going to come and it will be your job to send them on their way if you are not ready. The whole person is much more functional then the broken person. Yes, you can function being broken, but at what cost? What capacity and for how long before breaking again?

The process is for you to first fix the things that are broken in you, second to restore and realign the things in your life that needs it and third to make you a better you. Anything that has been broken will have gaps, holes, cracks and leaks in it. Therefore, leaving room for nothing or not much to be held. A person capacity to hold, withstand, endure, relate, communicate, and their emotional strength and ability wouldn't be at their best, without first making the proper repairs. Your focus should be on what really matters. Handle first things first and that is you and your well-being.

Key Questions to Ask:

- Do you matter to you, if so how much?

- Are you willing to put in the work without any distractions?

- Are you willing to work on you first?

- Are you willing to not make any excuses?

- Do you value or love yourself regardless of what you are going through or what you have been through?

- Do you believe in you?

- Are you ready to take ownership of putting your life back together?
  _____
  _____
  _____

- Are you willing to be open minded in your healing process to do every and all things necessary to restore you?
  _____
  _____
  _____

- Are you willing to take a vow to yourself that no matter how long your process takes you won't give up on you?
  _____
  _____
  _____

- Are you willing to carry out your process regardless of how you look?
  _____
  _____
  _____

- Are you willing to carry out your process regardless of who you may lose along the way?
  _____
  _____
  _____

- Are you willing to carry out your process no matter the cost?
  _____
  _____
  _____

- Do you like and love you enough to put you back together again?

  _____
  _____
  _____

- Are you willing and ready to examine you and your faults?

  _____
  _____
  _____

- Are you willing and ready to be honest with you?

  _____
  _____
  _____

Now you add some of your own questions or thoughts

Key Factors to Remember:

- Be mindful of the things that should matter or shouldn't matter
- Be ok with opening the necessary wounds for you to be healed
- Remember some wounds will hurt more than others but take one day and one step at a time
- Remember some truths will hurt more than others but continue your process
- Keep an open mind that although you may have given a lot to the relationship or marriage their still could've been some things done differently on your part to safe guard you
- Remember that your healing isn't about showing how naive of a person that you were it is to show you what damage was caused within self and where the work needs to be done
- Remember not to beat yourself up don't further damage yourself
- Remember to allow the proper time to grieve but don't live in the grieving stage for months or years
- Allow yourself to Let it out and Let it go
- Don't worry about how you look to others or what people think or the lies that have been told on you
- Don't live in a depressive state
- Remember in a break up or a divorce the other person will paint the picture that looks most beautiful for him or her
- Don't be so concern about telling your side or your story because your silence and light will shine at the appropriate time and those who have eyes to see, they will see and if they don't, be ok with it

Let Go

Letting go will free you. However, letting go will be one of the hardest things in your process that you will have to work through. If you have spent any significant amount of time with your ex, then you will find yourself reminiscing over the good and bad memories that you built with your ex. You may find yourself thinking about the sexually bond that you had with your ex or the different levels of intimacy that you had grown accustom to receiving before it all stopped. Also, you may find yourself reflecting over the things they would do rather they were good or bad.

For some, you will continue to replay what could have been done differently. What good times you had with your ex, why did the marriage or relationship stop working and if they left you for someone else, then your thoughts would be, why? From time to time you may oftentimes think about what made the other person a better choice than you, if that was your issue. Nevertheless, the longer you hold on to the what if's and what could have been done differently and the whys, then it will take that much longer for you to get over your ex.

When you hold on to the pain and hurt and you keep replaying different scenarios in your mind you will only slow your process of healing down. There are stages to healing and the grievance process is one. Most people want closure; but the truth of the matter is; it is rare that you are going to get an answer that will give you the proper closure that is needed. If you were to get the answer to the why, you problem wouldn't want it or you couldn't accept it. The other person truth will more than likely be filled with more lies or with responses of, I don't know.

You will need to work on getting to a place where you are not looking for your ex to give you closure because to be honest you are not going to get a truthful answer anyway. If they gave you the truth, could you honestly handle it? You are going to have to give yourself closure and that closure is going to come by you taking one day at a time and one step at a time and letting go of everything that was associated to the previous relationship or marriage. No one said it is going to be easy but each day as time goes on you will began to feel a little better. Each day as you let go you will begin to heal a little more and a little more.

I want you to keep in mind a couple of things, if someone can walk away from you; then that wasn't the person that was meant for you to do life with. If you walked away from your ex, then that wasn't the person that was meant for you to do life with. Anyone that is meant to be in your life, please believe that they will be around for the long haul, meaning to death do you apart, if those were the vows that you and your significant other had legally shared.

Also, if you were married then they would have honored the marriage and the vows that you both took. Their stay wouldn't be temporary or short-term because they would have known and you would have known that the purpose in which you decided to be together is bigger than a short-term or temporary stay. I know that it is easier said than done when you talk about letting go, but letting go is to free you, even if you were the one that walked away.

I've learned that if you hold on to a person that doesn't want to be held, it only hurts you. Also, you will find out really fast how much stress and unnecessary pains and body aches that you will put your body through. You will also find out how many restless and sleepless nights you will continue to have by not letting go. Not letting go will cause for you to be in a restless place instead of a peaceful place.

Stop giving thoughts to someone who could care less about you or your well-being. If someone can leave you for whatever the reason is, let them go! If you left someone for whatever the reason was, be ok with your decision and know that going back or holding on to a lie is only going to end at some point; so don't prolong the pain.

One of the many concerns that some people have is, I don't know how to start over or let go. Which is common, this is why I said allow yourself to go through the process of healing, yes it will hurt; I am not going to tell you that it doesn't because it does. Letting go will hurt before it feels better, there isn't any other way to put it. It hurts because you had a soul-tie to your ex and for others a sexual bond and time that was shared.

Cutting hurts and separation hurts, I wish that I can say it will be easy; but what I can say is if you put in the work and give yourself the time and closure that you need to move forward, in time you will feel good again. If you continue to harbor the pain and hurt and keep pressing the rewind button in your mind over the pain, memories or sexual encounters, then you will only allow yourself to stay in bondage to your ex longer then you need to be. Obviously, there wasn't enough good memories or good times to keep the marriage or relationship together in a healthy manner. Let go and start loving and living life for you!

Key Questions to Ask:

- Was the marriage or relationship healthy, if not why?

- If it was meant for your ex to be with you then why did they leave or why did you leave?

- Do you have a support team or person to assist you while you are going through your process of letting go?

- Do you feel embarrassed or ashamed and if so why?

- Are you constantly reflecting over memories about your ex, if so why?

- Do you feel depressed; What are your fears?

- Are you reading or watching videos that can assist in your healing process?

  _____
  _____
  _____

- What are you doing daily that is bringing you to your place of healing?

  _____
  _____
  _____

- Have you started the process of disconnecting from your ex, if not why?

  _____
  _____
  _____

- If you don't have any children together have you gone no contact so that you can heal without allowing access to you?

  _____
  _____
  _____

- If you can't go completely no contact do you make the conversations short and to the point?

  _____
  _____
  _____

- Have you blocked your ex from your social media sites and possibly some friends or have you deactivated your social sites for a short period of time?

  _____
  _____
  _____

- Have you set down with yourself to think about a daily plan as to how life looks for you?

  _____
  _____
  _____

- Have you taken the focus and your thoughts off of what people might say?

  _____
  _____
  _____

- Have you let go of the tears or are you holding them back?

  _____
  _____
  _____

- Do you know that you are more than a wife or a husband or a girlfriend or boyfriend?

  _____
  _____
  _____

- Can you really whole heartily be with someone that you don't trust or you stop believing in?

  _____
  _____

Now you add some of your own questions or thoughts

Key Factors to Remember:

- You are more then what you are going through
- Letting go hurts but holding on to someone that isn't healthy hurts even more
- Starting over hurts but being in a relationship or a marriage that isn't healthy is just as bad
- Let go and believe that God has someone or something better in store for you
- Marriage is beautiful when done right
- Being single is amazing when done right
- Be ok when you have to walk away from someone that is no longer good for you
- Nothing toxic is good or going to produce anything good
- Love you and pick the pieces up with dignity and humility
- Your heart is a fragile vessel, don't allow anyone to abuse it
- If you left remember you left for a reason
- If your ex left you remember he or she wasn't meant to do life with you if they chose to walk away from you
- Stop thinking with your heart and allow your heart to heal
- Love yourself back to health
- The facts are what they are, remember the truth will set you free
- Lies only create more lies which create distrust
- You can come out of this on top (meaning healthy) but you first have to believe that you can; renew your mind of what you told yourself about the things that you can't do
- You only get one life but you can start over as many times as it takes

No Contact

No contact is sometimes hard especially when you are use to having contact with someone who you have once cared about. This can be extremely harder if you still care about your ex or if you are still in love with your ex-partner. Having no contact should mainly be put in place so that you can heal in peace without the distractions from your ex-partner. Also, if you have left the relationship or marriage because of any form of abuse, having no contact allows you the necessary time and space to find you again.

Having no contact isn't about playing a mind game with your ex, it's about you being free to devote the time and effort into yourself. No contact allows you to put your life back together in a way that works for you. Are you going to have moments where you think about your ex-partner, for some, yes? Are you going to have days where you may miss your ex, for some yes? Are you going to feel weak and vulnerable where you are going to want to call your ex, or want to see your ex, or maybe even sleep with your ex, for some yes?

All of these things are natural because you built a bond with your ex and now that the bond or the unit has taken on division and a separate direction the separation of the unit feels the backlash of the pain and the hurt. It feels like a wound that is open and it is taking forever to heal or to close. No contact will take discipline. I say this because occasionally a person falls weak to going back to their ex several times before they can totally walk away. This can happen when a person still has hope deferred that things can be better or that something is going to be different. This is not the case for all because each marriage or relationship is different depending on how the breakup or divorce ended.

Having no contact means just that. It means no calling and if you do have to communicate having less communications as possible and only talk about what is of importance. This doesn't mean that you set yourself up for the small conversations of how have you been? Is there anything I can do for you, if so call me? Having no contact means, no sex, no dinner dates, no going out to the movies, not being friends on social media, not going places where your ex-partner will be, also it can mean not hanging around some of the same friends. If you are going to go no contact, you have to do this all the way because if you don't you will only be cheating yourself out of your own personal healing.

You will also be allowing your ex-partner to play games with you because you have left the door opened or cracked where he or she can come in and out as they please. This is one of the many reasons that it takes some people longer to heal, because they allow themselves to still be accessible to their ex-partner. Is having no contact going to be easy starting off, no; but each day it will get better over time. To be honest, it will hurt before it gets better, but it will get better.

Everyday isn't going to be dark, there will be a light at the end of the tunnel, but you have to first take the steps to get to the light. Each time that you go back into a broken relationship or marriage and you leave and go back and leave and go back, the pain doesn't get easier it is still going to hurt if not worst. Having no contact allows you the ability to be restored back to a healthy state of being so that you can rebuild the things that you lost that is needed for your own personal healing. Sometimes you don't realize what you lost or all that you lost until you have actually left the relationship or marriage.

Will you find yourself having sleepless nights, but of course you will because your body and mind has to adjust to your new normal of no longer being with your ex. This is a lifestyle change and anytime you make a lifestyle change it is not something to be done temporarily; it is for life. Remember having no contact isn't about you being controlling, it's about you taking your control back and building a new life for yourself without your ex. It is so easy to keep falling back into the same trap of dysfunction when you don't follow and maintain an exit plan to having no contact.

No contact is to self-guard you so that you can stay on the right track for what works for you; it's not for or about the other person, it is all about you. You have to get out of the role of being the caregiver so that you can be cared for. Your new role is called self-care. Meaning it is now time for you to care for self so that you can be healed. No contact allows you to take the time to stop your own bleeding, pain and hurt so that you can regain who you are again as a person and individual without having the attachment that you once had with your ex. Be encouraged and start your no contact even if it hurts.

Key Questions to Ask:

- What's really holding you back from going no contact?

- What are you still holding on to?

- Why do you feel you still want to have contact with your ex-partner?

- Is it healthy for you to have contact with your ex-partner, if so why?

- Are you ready to take the steps of no contact, if not why?

- Do you feel alone?

- Would you feel shameful if you went to a support group, if so why?

  _____
  _____
  _____

- Do you still want to be with your ex, if so why?

  _____
  _____
  _____

- Why is it hard for you to let go?

  _____
  _____
  _____

- Do you believe that having contact with your ex-partner is healthy while you are trying to heal?

  _____
  _____
  _____

- What are some of your triggers when you hear or see your ex?

  _____
  _____
  _____

- Are you making excuses to still have a reason to communicate or see your ex?

  _____
  _____
  _____

- Do you care about yourself enough to want to press the reset button for your own life?

- Are you ready to love you without any negative thoughts of being alone?

- Did you know that once you have been in a relationship or marriage that has been full of take, take, take and no give, you will find your strength to be depleted?

- Are you willing to go the extra mile for you?

- Are you ready to stretch your way back to health, even if it hurts?

Now you add some of your own questions or thoughts

Key Factors to Remember:

- Having no contact isn't a bad thing it just allows you the necessary time to heal

- Somethings are hard but worth it in the end, especially when it comes to self-care

- Don't short change yourself because of fear

- There is never a really good time or bad time to start something, the one thing that stands in the way of starting anything is the mindset and the willingness of the person to start and finish

- Remember that you have to start somewhere so why not with you

- Don't wait on someone to give you permission to be healed, take what you need for you

- Find your own reason to live again, even if it means being alone

- Don't continue to give your power and control to your ex by living a life filled with guilt, live your life, if you don't know what your life is; then find it, it's not too late

- Don't be afraid to birth new things or build new things because you still have great and wonderful things inside of you

- Remember all is not lost, somethings just have to be reset

- Don't look at age or the time lost, look at it as lessons that were learned and teach from your place of pain and heal others once you have been healed, because you are not the only one that can heal from your place of pain

- Don't allow this experience to steal from you but take all of the pain, hurt and suffering and teach and give it to the next man or woman who maybe going through what you have gone through or already have gone through; there is healing in sharing your pain

- You can do no contact and anything else that you put your mind too

How do I Love Me Again?

Loving you first starts with self-love, self-healing, self-worth, self-esteem, self-care and learning to value you again. Self-love opens the door for you to explore yourself. One of the requirements will be, is that you will have to take the focus off the other person and focus on you. What I mean by focus on you is, you have to look at the things within yourself that have gotten broken or wounded and began the work to repair the damage. Oftentimes this is the work that either a person doesn't want to do or they don't take the proper time to finish the process to love them again. No one wants to sit with the pain or hurt, for many people they either don't deal with the pain at all and for others they tend to jump into another relationship or marriage taken the broken pieces of them into the next relationship or marriage.

Loving yourself is really going to require you to put in the work. Once you take the time to start the work of learning how to love you again, what you will stumble across is, where your brokenness is and how much repair will need to be done for you to truly love yourself again. Now loving yourself doesn't require for you to be this new vain person where everything is about you, but what the work will show is that you love yourself enough to the point that you won't allow anyone to hurt, abuse, misuse, or mistreat you. It will also show that you have taken the time to fix the broken things within you so that others won't have the entry to play on a weakness that you may have not been aware of or you just didn't take the time to fix.

Loving yourself is also going to require that you spend time alone, this is often hard for many people to do. Most people battle with the fear of being alone, unfortunately this process of healing and starting over is going to require that you not rush into another relationship or marriage until you have done the work on yourself first. When you began to walk through the process of loving yourself one of the many things that you will learn is, to pay more attention to the red flags and to let go sooner. Also you will learn not to enter into the next relationship or marriage with a sense of urgency. When you genuinely love yourself, you won't accept pain from someone who keeps on hurting you. Loving you requires that you protect your heart when the person that you have chosen to share it with keeps hurting you without any remorse. Loving yourself also requires that you don't settle for someone who really doesn't care for you or have your best interest at heart.

One of my own personal lessons that I have learned about when you love yourself is, you won't keep allowing yourself to keep going around and around in a circle making or accepting the same mistakes with the same person or with a different person that only ends up hurting you. Sometimes people can see the fragileness or the brokenness in you even when you can't. This is why when you start to do the work of loving yourself it will require that you examine yourself emotionally, physically and mentally. Don't short change yourself when it comes to learning how to love you again. Don't be concerned with being with someone else before you actually put in the work that is needed for you.

How do you stop the hurting, the pain and the internal bleeding; by doing the necessary self-work. True rehabilitation starts and ends with you. True recovery starts with you. It's time that you nurture your own wounds back to health. Stop taking short cuts when it comes to you. There are no excuses for you not to put in the work of self-love, other than you have made the choice to stay wounded and you chose to ignore that you are the one who now needs help. When you have been the person who has been the giver, you don't realize when you need help or when you are running on fumes or when you are depleted.

Starting over allows you to be restored, refueled, rejuvenated, replenished, and realigned. Starting over also allows you to reinvent yourself into a better version of you. Don't be afraid to love you again and if you have never loved you this is a good time while you are starting over to learn to love you. What do you have to lose? Loving you isn't about who should you blame or what you didn't get, it is truly about loving you. I dare you to seek how it looks and feel to genuinely love you.

Key Questions to Ask:

- What's holding you back from starting over?

  _____
  _____
  _____

- Are you ready to start self-love and if not why?

  _____
  _____
  _____

- Are you ready to put in the time, effort, and sacrifice to heal and discover true self-love?

  _____
  _____
  _____

- Are you ready to let go of what you knew about love and learn and upgrade your mind with some new tools?

  _____
  _____
  _____

- Are you focusing on what others may think or say or are you working on your new image?

  _____
  _____
  _____

- Are you ready to seek and fix the broken things that are within you?

- Do you love yourself, if so on a scale of 1-10 what is your number?

- Do you know your ends? Meaning, when something needs to come to an end?

- Have you given up on you?

- Do you feel like you are stuck in the phase of I don't know, what if or Why?

- Do you know that starting over hurts but you can get through it?

- Are you ready to be free in your mind and in your heart?

  _____
  _____
  _____

- Do you believe that you can do this regardless of what you have told yourself?

  _____
  _____
  _____

- Do you believe in you?

  _____
  _____
  _____

Now you add some of your own questions or thoughts

Key Factors to Remember:

- Starting over to explore self-love can be both painful but yet beautiful

- Don't look at self-love as though you never had love for yourself, look at it as though you are getting a tune-up

- If you never loved yourself then look at the process as knowledge to better yourself

- In life we are not always going to get things right, but if we learn from the mistakes then we can take the mistakes as lessons learned

- When life squeezes you or comes by to test you, don't fold, don't give up, but get back up bigger, better and stronger

- Tell yourself this, I am not what I have been through and my mistakes doesn't define who I am as a person and as I keep living I will make more mistakes but I vow to make less of them in the same areas of life

- I am a good person who have experienced a level or levels of pain in my life that I won't allow to break me but to build me into becoming my best person

- When situations in life knock me down I will get back up and keep conquering, overcoming and fighting for the better and best me possible

- I am an imperfect person who will live my life daily seeking to be better and to be the best person of who I was created to be

- Don't deprive yourself of living your best life no matter how old you are, no matter how long it takes, no matter what other people may say

- Everything that you have gone through in life wasn't meant to break you; there is light at the end, you just can't give up

- Love you, respect you and never allow others to make you optional to love,

Picking Up the Piece's

When you think about picking up the pieces one of the first questions that comes to mind is how? One thought that will come to mind is; I don't know how it would look to do this walk alone. After coming out of a marriage or relationship things may appear really blurred and you may even find yourself in a place of confusion, asking the question; how did I get here? There are so many different thoughts that will run through your mind before you get to the place of picking up the pieces.

Picking up the pieces is a short term for where do I start, what piece of my life do I have the strength to start on first. So many different things will begin to race through your mind when you think about picking up the pieces to the point where it can become overwhelming. Picking up the pieces will look different for everyone. You will have to take an evaluation and do a self-assessment of the damage that has been done. One of the many things that you will discover in the process of picking up the pieces is; you will have to work on several things at one time. During this process depending on how the relationship or marriage ended this can and will be a struggle to start your process of picking up the pieces.

You will oftentimes find yourself having to deal with your emotions while also having to deal with the business side of the marriage or relationship. In this process your head is still foggy, sometimes mistakes are made because you don't have the mental or physical strength to fight the many things that you will face when leaving the relationship or marriage. There may be confrontation around kids, money, living situation, vehicles, joints accounts, and so much more. In this process you will oftentimes find yourself struggling to find your ends and your starting point.

Picking up the pieces is what I call a double sword. It cuts and prunes while building and restoring. The real work of picking up the pieces starts after the ripping. Some of the work is done while in the storm but the majority of the work will be done once you are in a more calming place after dealing with the constant warfare and issues that pertained to your ex. Once you are able to put your mind in a more stable and quieter place; picking up the pieces will challenge you to make the choice to live again as a single person and arrange your life according. It will also challenge you to look ahead and not at the things that are behind you.

You won't get very far if you keep your focus on the things that happened in your last marriage or relationship. Picking up the pieces means just that, pick up what pieces that are an essential need for you to start over and the things that are not then leave them behind. There are pieces such as holding on to old memories of your ex, old behavior patterns, along with entertaining old friends or going to old places and having unnecessary conversations with your ex; are all things that shouldn't be a part of your new journey of picking up the pieces.

These habits will only hinder your personal growth and your process of you starting over in becoming a healthier and better you. One thing that you should know about broken pieces are; they will reveal what pieces were the wrong pieces and what pieces are the right pieces to allow on your new journey. No process is simple and everything comes with some level of work. If you don't allow the broken pieces to define you and you whole heartily work on building and putting you back together again, I guarantee that the new pieces of you will shine and smile again.

Don't allow yourself to be defeated or broken to the point that you don't get back up. Take one piece at a time until the pieces fit the way that is pleasing to you. Don't take all the broken pieces from your last relationship or marriage, leave room for the new pieces to grow. Learn from the broken pieces, thrive and flourish from all pieces, but don't carry the weight of your old into your new. Dead weight only weighs you down, make this go around light for the flight so that you can have a smoother take off then the last place you left.

Key Questions to Ask:

- Do you know the things that are broken within you?

- Are you still holding on to the broken pieces?

- Are you ready to work on you?

- Have you taken the time to think about how to pick up the pieces?

- Do you feel overwhelmed, if so why?

- Do you feel like picking up the pieces are impossible, if so why?

- Can you see yourself being a better person since you are not with your ex?
  _____
  _____
  _____

- Do you feel that you are in a tough place and if so why?
  _____
  _____
  _____

- What are three feelings that you have in this very moment?
  _____
  _____
  _____

- What are you telling yourself about your current situation?
  _____
  _____
  _____

- Are you speaking words of affirmation to yourself daily?
  _____
  _____
  _____

- What steps have you taken if any since departing from your ex that has proven to be a positive growth factor in your life?
  _____
  _____
  _____

Now you add some of your own questions or thoughts

Key Factors to Remember:

- Picking up the pieces isn't about what you can't do but it is about the strength, growth and character of you starting over again

- Don't be ashamed to start your process because of what others may say or because of who may be watching you

- Don't allow other people to validate your life, don't give others a say in your life, because your life is just that, Your Life

- Sometimes when your life has been chosen to play out before the world it can feel embarrassing and rewarding all at the same time.

- The pieces can and will change you but allow your pieces to change you for the better not for the worst

- Don't get tired when it comes to putting your puzzle back together, take a break when you need to but don't stop investing in you, don't stop caring for you and most importantly don't give up on you

- Remember you are so worth the work, don't you want to see the finish product, however that might look

- Remember this, when you remove your whole self from all the mess that was hindering you, and you began to plant new roots, then and only then will you see your life began to grow

- Let the old go so that you can walk into your new

The Stigma Behind Divorce

Divorce rates are higher now than ever before. People marry for many different reasons. It is safe to say that people also divorce for many different reasons. Some would say; they just grew apart, others would say their divorce was because of infidelity, selfishness, or mental or physical distress, emotional, or sexual abuse, while others would say their reason was because of greed, mistrust, narcissistic abuse and the list can go on and on. I don't believe that anyone enters into a marriage with the intention of getting a divorce. I believe that the majority of people who get married have the belief that they have found their partner to do life with until death do them apart.

Divorce is hard, because it comes with some legal matters that both parties have to go through in order to be legally separated. It's not something that you can walk away from and not have a legal tie to the other person. Especially if there are kids involved, property or money that has to be divided. Sometimes both parties are able to come into an agreement which will end the divorce faster. But then there are other times where the two parties can't agree upon anything which causes for the divorce to take longer. Either way it doesn't take away the pain and stigma behind getting a divorce.

Some people have been married once and they have made up in their mind that once was enough. Then you have others who have been married up to six or seven times who still believes in marriage. It doesn't really matter how many times that a person has been married because society still views marriage as it should only be done one time no matter the situation. This is where the shame comes in at, because for those of you who have been married multiple times for whatever your reason, society has deemed you to be foolish if you marry more than once or twice.

You may have heard things like you are a broken human being or your judgement of people isn't very good. You may have even heard things like you haven't spent enough time by yourself to heal before you entered into another marriage or you don't have enough self-love and this is why you keep marrying the wrong person, or you didn't ask the right questions, which these things could be true to a degree. However, that might not have been the cause for your divorce. There is so much disapproval and judgement placed on divorce to the point where people don't care about the well-being of a person. There is more emphasis placed on condemning and shaming someone for wanting a divorce then there is for the health and overall good of a person. You can't change the actions or non-actions of another individual, you can only change you.

Whatever the reason is that your marriage had to be dissolved don't allow others to shame you for it. Always remember when you said your vows a covenant was made between you and your ex-spouse not with the world, friends, family or outsiders. Remember that you granted access for some people to witness your covenant, but that doesn't give anyone the right to attest or disprove of the dissolution of your marriage. Marriages end for so many reasons as I stated before.

Oftentimes you will learn that the person who you married wasn't who they professed to be. You may also find out that your partner didn't disclose of a mental health condition, or any addictions they might have had. If you have been married for any long period of time, your spouse may have made a change for the worst. Again there are so many reasons as to the why, but whatever your reason; don't allow anyone to shame you because you decided to get a divorce. You owe no one no explanation about what happened or what didn't happen in your marriage.

Life and people will take you on so many rides; to the point where you will sometimes feel like you are on a rollercoaster ride that won't stop. Don't be concerned about what people have to say more than you are making sure that you are in a healthy place mentally, physically, spiritually and emotionally. People are going to talk; they wouldn't be people if they didn't. Look around the world, people have given themselves the right to comment or say whatever they want rather right or wrong or good or bad. If you get caught up in the noise of what others have to say you won't make the right decision for you.

No matter how many times you have been married or the reasons behind the divorce/s, remember people make mistakes so don't judge yourself harshly or make a lifelong ruling over your life because of what others think, feel or believe. Marriage is a beautiful thing when done right, but it most definitely has to be done with the right person, meaning someone that you are equally yoked with. Marriage is just like anything else, its takes work and it requires maintenance and repairs ever so many miles. It requires new data and uploads along with a tune-up of new ideas, it will also require you to be a forever dater. Don't beat yourself up about the divorce, but allow yourself to grow from the mistakes and use them as lessons learned.

Don't allow people to shame you as though their life is perfect and they have it all together, because if you were to take a peek in their window you would see their imperfections that they struggle with. Stop carrying around the shame that is associated with divorce and drop off its partner regret. Life happens, things happen, but don't allow divorce to define who you are as a person, rather you have experienced one divorce or multiple.

Key Questions to Ask:

- Are you carrying around the shame of your divorce/s, if so why?
  _____
  _____
  _____

- What lessons have you learned from your divorce?
  _____
  _____
  _____

- Have you started the process in which it will take to heal?
  _____
  _____
  _____

- Are you judging yourself too harshly?
  _____
  _____
  _____

- Have you moved on mentally from being married?
  _____
  _____
  _____

- What are you doing to heal from the damage of the divorce?
  _____
  _____
  _____

- Are you ready to work on you?

  _____
  _____
  _____

- Do you still believe in marriage and if not why?

  _____
  _____
  _____

- Would you get married again?

  _____
  _____
  _____

- If you have done the work, do you believe that you know what red flags to look for as it pertains to marriage or entering into a marriage?

  _____
  _____
  _____

- Did you seek counseling before you got married?

  _____
  _____
  _____

- Do you care what people are saying or have said, if so why?

  _____
  _____
  _____

- Did you attend any divorce groups or have you talked to a life coach or therapist or counselor?

  _____
  _____
  _____

- What are your feelings or thoughts about marriage?

  _____
  _____
  _____

- How do you feel about starting over?

  _____
  _____
  _____

Now you add some of your own questions or thoughts

Key Factors to Remember:

- People are going to be people but don't stop being who you are

- You can't control what people might say but you can control your thoughts and what you chose to entertain or speak on

- Remember a marriage doesn't define your total being as a person and neither does a divorce

- Sometimes the intentions of a person start off good but end up later being bad

- No one can predict if they truly have the right person in whom they said I Do to, you can only hope or pray for the best

- You can't change people but you can always make the choice to do the self-work so that you can become a better you

- When you have given and given and given and given and when you think that you don't have anything else to give, reach down deeper and find the strength to give to self

- Heal from within and do it for yourself not for anyone else

- When you are not in a good place then you are no longer any good to yourself or anyone else

- Going through a divorce hurts, it's painful, shameful, and undeniable hard, but it isn't anything that you can't get through

- I know you didn't sign up for divorce on your wedding day but you can make the choice to start over, the choice is up to you and no one else

- Don't waste too much time dwelling on the divorce allow yourself the proper time to grieve and heal

- Date You, Love You, Get to know You, and Spend time with You

Learning To Identify Your Strength And Weaknesses

Starting over is never easy, learning to identify your strength and weaknesses after coming out of a relationship or marriage isn't easy either. You will oftentimes find yourself in a place where you will have to rebuild and repair and identify new strengths. Also, you will discover new weaknesses mixed with previous weaknesses that will require you to work on. This process isn't always easy but it is worth it.

Oftentimes you will find out; when you have been in a relationship or marriage for a period of time and you have invested so much of yourself, it is easy to lose yourself and relax some of the boundaries that were put in place to protect you from the things seen or not seen. It's like you almost have to relearn to identify the very things that were strong about you. Over time you may have learned that the things that made you strong now act as a weakness in your life or vice versa. You may also learn that you may have picked up some new weaknesses. This is why you have to take the time for yourself to assess the damage and your level of strength.

There is no easy way realistically to identify your strength and weaknesses unless you do the work. When you are broken it places you in a blind spot where you are partially able to see. The brokenness screams fix me and I don't care how you fix me, but do it and do it now; but you say, no, because it hurts to bad. Then the practical and healthier side says; endure the process and heal in all areas and lets not take any short cuts. Now you get into this toggle war that says, I don't want to feel the pain, and how long does this suppose to last for? Which later only ends up being bad for you because you will find yourself with a temporary fix that will eventually end up to be a long term problem as well as a constant problem; because you never took the time to repair the brokenness or evaluated your strength and or weaknesses.

Everything bad isn't always bad if you can look at it and find a reason to grow from it. You can learn from the bad things instead of allowing it to affect you in a negative way. The choice is yours but remember, you do have a choice and all isn't lost. Don't allow the bad to break you, instead allow it to build you and develop a better, stronger and healthier person. One thing about starting over is, it doesn't favor any one person, but the person will have to make the choice to want to start over.

Don't talk yourself out of being healed because being in a broken state doesn't benefit you or anyone else. Even if you have decided that you don't want to be in another relationship or get married again, the work still needs to be done so that you can have peace within yourself. The trauma has to be addressed in order for you to fix any problem. Ignoring or denying that there was any damage done only keeps you in a dysfunctional and unhappy place. Don't be afraid to identify your weakness, brokenness, pain, hurt or fears. Strength is the quality or state of being physically strong but to go further than that, allow strength to also build you mentally and emotionally and spiritually.

Key Questions to Ask:

- If you were to rate your worth on a scale from 1-10 what would it be, 10 being the highest?

- Do you believe in you?

- Do you have hope that things can have a better outcome then where they are now?

- Are you willing to learn and grow regardless of what you currently believe or see?

- How do you see yourself?

- Do you know your strengths?

  _____
  _____
  _____

- Do you know your weaknesses?

  _____
  _____
  _____

- Do you find yourself lying to yourself and pretending to be happy?

  _____
  _____
  _____

- Do you feel like you are constantly in a state of anxiety?

  _____
  _____
  _____

- Are you being strong in front of others but silently breaking down when you are alone?

  _____
  _____
  _____

- Do you feel like you are too tired to do the work needed for you?

  _____
  _____
  _____

- Have you created balance in your life or are you filling your time up with stuff or things to do that doesn't bring forth true healing?

  _____
  _____
  _____

- Have you taken the time to decide what areas of your life that needs to be worked on first, second, third and so on?

  _____
  _____
  _____

Now you add some of your own questions or thoughts

Key Factors to Remember:

- When everyone says no tell yourself yes

- Remember this is a stage in your life but it isn't the end of your life

- Remember that everyone has weaknesses and the work is to repair the brokenness and strengthen the weaknesses one day and one step at a time

- Remember we all are going to have some level of weakness but being able to identify what they are keeps us in a better and healthier place

- Not knowing your strength and weaknesses can be dangerous because it leaves you to be open and vulnerable where a person has the potential to do harm to you

- Learning your ends and growing in stability only helps you to be your best person

- Walk with your head up and lead with the power that lives within and if you don't know the power that you have, this is a good time to learn

- Don't allow fear to convince you that you shouldn't fight to be healed or that you should give up on yourself

- Be strong even if you feel weak, be courageous even when you feel uncertain, be fearless even when you feel fearful

- Remember that a person may have taken a piece of you but the best pieces of you still remains with you

- Tap into your greatness, press into your best parts and evolve into the Queen or King that you were created to be

- Be creative and reinvent and rediscover the best of you, it's in there, you just have to search for it

How To Move Forward Without Feeling A Sense Of Shame

Life happens and what you will learn is that no matter what you do; this thing called life will come to challenge or throw road blocks in your way with things that you didn't even plan for or would have never expected to happen. If you keep living or if you have lived for any amount of time then you will have already learned that life is a journey, it will take you up, down, around, back up and then balance you and then start all over again with the up and down and around. Sometimes life will make you feel as though you are on a merry go round that won't stop.

No one plans to have a miserable life or a nasty breakup or unsuccessful marriage. For the majority of people their hopes and dreams are to live a blissful, joyful, comfortable and serene life with the person in whom they chose to be their partner. Unfortunately, that doesn't always happen. When life throws a punch or hits you so hard that it feels like your air wave have been closed off, you began to wonder at that point; can I get back up from this or how do I get back up? If you have been in a relationship or in a marriage with your ex-partner for any number of years and you or them decided to call it quits, one of the many questions that always seems to come up is how shameful is this going to look to everyone else who thought that you were the perfect couple? The other question is, what will others think? You will especially feel a sense of shame if you are already on your 2nd, 3rd, 4th, or 5th marriage.

I want to let you know that it doesn't matter what your number is, what is most important is that you move forward in a healthy manner. Things happen, life happens, people change, people grow apart and so much more. If you were to be honest with yourself, if you were in a relationship or marriage that was toxic and full of drama or was emotionless, abusive, narcissistic or whatever the case was; how good was that for you and your overall mental, physical or emotion state? Sometimes people stay in a relationship or marriage way longer then they need to because of certain fears that they may have or either because they have deferred hope that that person is going to change or things are going to get better.

Nevertheless, when something has ran its course and there is nothing else to fuel it that breathes life, the only other solution is to dissolve it. If this is a choice that was made on your behalf or your ex-partner, respect the decision without looking at what and how much was invested. Don't allow a situation to drain you to the point that you have no life or energy left for yourself. Shame will come and shame will go, what matters is what you are telling yourself. What you are telling yourself is what you will believe, don't worry yourself about what other people may say or believe. Once you learn that we all come with human errors and we all have defects; then and only then, will you be ok with allowing yourself to fail or make mistakes without harshly judging yourself.

No one is perfect. One advice that I would recommend to you is to allow yourself to fail in order that you may learn. Also don't allow others to validate who you are as a person or your imperfections, flaws, or mistakes. Own what is yours and learn and grow in a healthy manner so that you can be better and not bitter. Shame can and will cause you to put up defenses that will allow nothing and nobody to get in or out. With every experience there should be a place of balance where you learn and grow.

When you are in a relationship or marriage it's not about how much or how fast you can give of yourself or do for someone else, it is about you being balanced in all that you do. Shame will come to bring you down, but if you allow shame to dictate your life, you will be too afraid to give any part of yourself to anyone because you will be afraid that you will be hurt. Your life isn't over you are just starting another chapter. Give yourself the freedom to close the last chapters so that you can open the new chapters.

Key Questions to Ask:

- What does shame mean to you?
  _____
  _____
  _____

- Do you know that everyone experience shame at some point in their life?
  _____
  _____
  _____

- Have you decided to press through the shame?
  _____
  _____
  _____

- What did you learn through this experience about yourself?
  _____
  _____
  _____

- What did you learn from the experience overall?
  _____
  _____
  _____

- How did this experience or how can this experience help you to grow?
  _____
  _____
  _____

- Are you going to allow yourself to fail without harshly judging yourself?

- Are you going to give yourself permission to move on?

- Do you know that holding on to shame stops you from living?

- Do you know that your life isn't over because of one failed experience?

- Are you going to take the steps to work through your painful emotions and your guilt?

- Do you know that love doesn't hurt, people hurt?

- Do you feel empty, if so why?

  _____
  _____
  _____

- Do you know that shame has no fear factor as to whom it will affect?

  _____
  _____
  _____

- Do you know that you are not alone although you may feel alone?

  _____
  _____
  _____

- Do you know that you are stronger then you see yourself?

  _____
  _____
  _____

Now you add some of your own questions or thoughts

Key Factors to Remember:

- Always remember that you have a choice even when you feel that you don't

- Remember that life isn't always going to be favorable or perfect or without storms or challenges

- Remember that you hold the power over yourself to come back from anything if you apply yourself

- Storms, barriers, challenges, hurts, pains, injustice, unfairness, being wronged, being stirred, being shaken, you name it that is something that many of us will experience in life

- Don't let what you have gone through change who you are as a person because ugly and nasty or bitter is not who you were created to be

- Life will deal you a hand that will sometimes have you asking the question of why, when that happens don't dwell on the why but press through to the end because you may never get the answer to the why

- Relationships and marriages are beautiful when done right and when two people both give of themselves and when both parties have the proper tools and resources to make it work

- Don't beat yourself up over a we or a us situation because you weren't in that relationship or marriage by yourself, don't waste time judging or blaming

- Remember that it was two parties involved and the mistakes came from both parties and if the relationship or marriage was to work, it would have had to come from both parties involved

Caring For You In A Healthy Manner

You give so much of yourself when you are in a marriage or relationship and sometimes that can cause you to lose who you are as an individual. You can get so busy in caring for the other person needs or wants and everything else that comes with being with that person to the point you didn't realize how draining or exhausting the marriage or relationship really was, especially if you add kids into the equation. Caring for you in a healthy manner means just that. After you have left the marriage or relationship you will have to figure out how to care for yourself again.

Caring for you may be difficult at first because for many of you, you gave so much of yourself until you lost the person who you once were before you entered into the marriage or relationship. If you were the type of person that took care of the majority of things or business while you were in the marriage or relationship, chances are you don't realize how depleted you are. You can't keep giving and giving and giving and never receive back. You also can't keep giving without never receiving back on the level that fits your needs. Oftentimes we give and give and give until there is nothing left or very little left for ourselves.

Marriage or being in a committed relationship isn't never about how much you can give, but it is about the shared responsibility and giving to one another. Ask yourself this question, what good is it if you are the only one who keeps being the one to forgive, serve, care for, cater to, or love in spite of; if that person isn't reciprocating that back. When someone shows you to be a deficit verses an asset you have to reevaluate the purpose of the union. You don't keep giving time and energy to something or someone that is only taking. Caring for yourself isn't about spending years in a marriage or relationship that you see isn't healthy or fruitful for both parties.

Caring for yourself, is you knowing when something is unbalanced and off and fixing it or addressing the matter so that you can come to a healthy resolution. You can save yourself a lot of heartaches and pain when you are able to care for yourself before things get really out of hand. It doesn't matter if you leave the marriage or relationship early or later; you will still encounter the pain; it will just come later on in the relationship or marriage. Love others but always love you more. There is nothing wrong with giving a person the opportunity to change, grow or fix their brokenness. However; what is wrong, is when you waste countless years in something that you saw that wasn't getting any better or kept repeating itself again and again and again.

One thing that you can't get back in life is time, with that being said don't allow people to misuse your time or waste your time. Many people get upset once they have left the marriage or relationship because of the time that they have invested and they knew that they should have been walked away. Caring for yourself doesn't start when you leave the marriage or relationship. Caring for yourself takes place before you enter into a marriage or relationship and while you are in the relationship or marriage and even when you leave. Caring for yourself never stops, it stays on duty 24/7.

If you have stopped caring for yourself, it's never too late to pick up the pieces and start over. This time around practice caring for yourself at all times, you should never stop caring for yourself or sacrifice your health, well-being, peace, joy or happiness for someone else. To be honest, how you cared for yourself was one of the things that attracted your ex-partner to you. Your partner saw that you were attentive and caring to your own personal needs and that was something that they knew would also be of a benefit to them. Always love and care for you, don't leave yourself out of the equation or don't put yourself on the back burner while you meet the needs and wants of other's. Caring for you in a healthy manner means to always keep you first. One thing that you need to remember is, you will never be good to anyone else if you are not First good for you and to you. If you are not healthy and operating from a balanced place, then how good are you to yourself or anyone else. You are at your best when your needs are met and you are balanced and well-rounded mentally, physically, emotionally and spiritually.

Key Questions to Ask:

- Do you know how to care for yourself?
  _____
  _____
  _____

- Are you ready to work on building and caring for yourself?
  _____
  _____
  _____

- What does caring for yourself mean to you?
  _____
  _____
  _____

- What have you learned from this experience as it pertains to caring for yourself?
  _____
  _____
  _____

- Have you already beaten yourself up like 10,000 times or more about your faults and what you could have done differently and what you lost, if so why?
  _____
  _____
  _____

- Have you counted up what you have gained from the lesson of caring for yourself in a healthy manner?

  _____
  _____
  _____

- If you were to rate how you care for yourself in your present state from 1-10 what would your number be?

  _____
  _____
  _____

- Do you feel like you have been robbed and if so of what?

  _____
  _____
  _____

- How much did you play in the role of not caring for yourself, what is the percentage?

  _____
  _____
  _____

- If you were to be honest with yourself what is the number of the year you should have left the marriage or relationship? Example, 1st year, 2nd year, 10th year.

  _____
  _____
  _____

- What is the year that you actually left the marriage or relationship after staying when you realized you should have left?

  _____
  _____
  _____

Now you add some of your own questions or thoughts

Key Factors to Remember:

- Don't stop caring for yourself

- Always remember to put you first

- Don't deplete you to the point that you have nothing left for yourself

- Never be afraid to restore or rebuild yourself

- Care for yourself and love yourself always and never lose sight of the importance of caring for you

- Know when you are giving too much of yourself and learn to balance every area of your life

- Don't allow yourself to be a doormat for others to dust their feet on

- Love, care and give, but be balanced and make sure that it is being giving back in the way that satisfies your needs as well

- Remember that caring for yourself comes first and it stays on duty 24/7

- Don't be so eager to care for others and lose you

- Remember that you have givers and takers; be able to identify who you are with, if that person is a giver or a taker

- Takers do just that, they take and take and take until there is nothing left to take

- Remember you can start over because life sometimes will require you to close some chapters and write new ones

- You are never too old or too young to learn and rebuild your life, keep your heart strong and your mind stronger

What To Do When Bitterness And Anger Set In

I know what I am about to say is easier said than done, however; the answer that I am going to say is to, Let Go! I know, your thoughts are; how can I let go when you don't know the hurt that I feel or the pain that I am going through or the sacrifices that I have made. You don't know how I suffered with all of the humiliation and shame that my ex has caused me. You don't have a clue about all that I have been through with my ex and all of the mean, cruel, evil, manipulative and deceitful things that were done to me. I just suppose to let go as though it didn't happen or I don't hurt.

No, I am not saying that how you feel isn't justifiable, but what I am saying is don't live in that place of bitterness and anger. Those things will only destroy you not the other person. They are gone on about their life and could care less that you are holding on to those things. Holding on to things like resentment, bitterness, anger and hurt among others things; only hurts you and has the potential to make you sick if you continue to harbor and hold on to those feelings. It's ok to take a little time to grieve but don't spend years grieving over that situation. Holding on to negative emotions, pain and hurt is like Cancer eating and spreading through your body, it's not good or healthy. Holding on to the negative emotions will only break you down and stop you from healing and being restored back to a healthy place.

It steals your joy, peace, strength, happiness and your ability to move forward in life. Don't allow the bad or misfortunate things to rob you of your future. It's ok to have those feelings, but don't allow them to stagnate you from your healing or starting over. Remember starting over is never about the other person it is about you. Being bitter and angry is like poison, at some point it will affect you if you chose to hold on to it and not let go. Forgiveness isn't only about or for the other person; so much as it is for you. Forgiveness allows you to let go and free yourself so that you can live and be a better and healthier person. People think that forgiveness is all about the other person. That isn't all true, rather you forgive the other person or not the majority of people are going to go on living their life as they please and sometimes as though nothing happened, while you are still holding on to the hurt and pain and being bitter.

When you realize that love didn't hurt you but the person did and he or she wasn't no longer a good fit for you; then and only then will you be able to start your journey of healing. I've learned that every person isn't going to be like the last person and Love is beautiful when experienced with the right person. Holding on to bitterness and anger only hurts you and not the other person. Love yourself enough to walk through the process to heal yourself. No person is worth you living your life in pain and being miserable. Don't concentrate on all of the bad or allow your mind to be a tape recorder that has a broken rewind button that keeps replaying all of the bad stuff.

Press fast forward and press towards the mark, there are greater and better things in store for you, you just have to want it and not be afraid to start over. I know some of you may be thinking, I am too old to start over, don't look at it as starting over in that sense, look at it as choosing to live life again without the attachment of pain. Now for some of you who have given many years of your life to a marriage or relationship, make the rest of your life count for you. Don't focus so much on the number of years that you gave your ex, direct your time and new found energy towards you.

For those of you who have been in a marriage or relationship for a shorter period of time, don't give up on you and don't be afraid to pick yourself back up and rebuild a better healthier you. It is better sooner than later that you left. Again don't put all of your focus on the years or the amount of time; but focus on You and your Healing.

Key Questions to Ask:

- Are you bitter or angry, if so why?

- Have you allowed yourself to grieve?

- How much time has gone by that you have allowed yourself to grieve?

- Are you going to any kind of support groups, if not why? (online is an option)

- Are you so angry that you don't want to see yourself healed?

- Are you still holding on to the pain and hurt?

- What are some of the positive things that you are saying to yourself?
  _____
  _____
  _____

- What are some of the negative things that you are saying to yourself?
  _____
  _____
  _____

- What does forgiveness mean to you?
  _____
  _____
  _____

- Have you truly forgiven your ex?
  _____
  _____
  _____

- Have you forgiven yourself?
  _____
  _____
  _____

- What are you doing to keep your mind on positive things?
  _____
  _____
  _____

- Have you set up a positive routine for yourself?
  _____
  _____
  _____

Now you add some of your own questions or thoughts

Key Factors to Remember:

- Holding on to unforgiveness only hurts you

- Live a life filled with peace and joy

- No one is worth your peace, joy or happiness

- Bitterness and anger is like Cancer, it eventually kills and most definitely will harm you if you hold on to it for a long period of time

- No one knows the depth of your pain or the hurt that you feel but don't allow that to be the excuse that you don't press towards your healing

- There will be some people in life that will be able to identify with your pain and even your hurt, don't exclude them from assisting you because of shame

- Shame or Embarrassment can and will disable your growth, it can also stop your healing process before you start

- Remember this is your life and your story or testimony so don't allow other's to validate your steps or progress

- Remember to take baby steps until you can take big steps and bigger steps

- Change is a process nothing happens overnight embrace your process and learn who you are now that you are no longer with your ex; don't be afraid to spend time with you

- Much has been lost but remember to take the time to see all of what you have gained

- Don't allow the pain of it all to rob you of what you could have and who you are outside of your ex

- Remember Love is Beautiful when experienced with the Right Person

- You are worth so much more then what you can see right now regardless of how you feel or what has been said to you or about you

Living A Life Filled With Peace And Joy

After all of the turmoil, trauma, drama, restless and sleepless nights and the back and forth until your head feels like it was literally about to pop off of your shoulders, now that you are alone; how do you live a life filled with peace and joy? Simple; one day at a time. Embrace life being single, embrace the quietness and peace and allow yourself to enter into the joy that you once had before your ex. Don't allow loneliness to be a reason for you to not be filled with peace and joy. There is great power and strength in peace.

Sometimes you don't realize how much was taken from you until you have left a toxic, abusive or adulterous relationship or marriage. It's not until you have left that you will see how much of your peace and joy you were robbed of. Being in a toxic relationship or marriage disturbs the dwelling place where your thoughts and dreams are developed. Finding that place of peace can be hard for many reasons. When a situation or toxic environment or relationship has stolen your peace of mind or your ability to thrive it will be challenging for you to live a life filled with joy and peace. Noticed that I said challenging not impossible.

Everything in life is a process, you have to want to work the process in order to bring something back to its original state or to restore it back to a healthy place. Living a life filled with peace and joy isn't impossible, it's about how hard you are willing to work for it. When something has been stolen from you, it is your job to rebuild it, by taking one day at a time and one step at a time.

Sometimes we can put so much emphasis on the other person and their faults to the point we lose sight of what is important, which is your own personal healing. Peace can't enter in or be restored if you continue to hold on to all of the pain, hurt and bad things that happened when you were in a relationship or marriage with your ex. When you allow peace to be mandatory in your life then you won't be quick to allow confusion, dysfunction or anything else that is not of peace to dwell or be in your midst.

Living a life that is filled with peace and joy means that you will have to take time to learn what works for you and what doesn't. That will require for you to spend some time alone with yourself to learn you all over again. Things change within an individual when the bond of having someone has been broken or when there has been a detachment. You have to not only work the process but also decide that peace and joy is something that you want. Living a life filled with peace and joy will require something from you and it is called sacrifice. The sacrifice is for you to put in the work so that you can become a healthier and better you.

You have a choice even when it looks like you don't. According to the Merriam Webster Dictionary it states, Peace is a state in which there is no war or fighting, a state of tranquility or quiet, freedom from disquieting or oppressive thoughts or emotions, harmony in personal relations. It also states that Joy is; a feeling of great happiness, a source or cause of delight, to experience great pleasure or delight. These things are often lost when you have gone through the ups and downs caused by being in an unhealthy relationship or marriage.

Living a life filled with peace and joy starts with you renewing your mind and giving yourself the opportunity to have a fresh start. Take the time to build yourself up again and grow in ways that you never imagined.

Of course no one wants to start over or keep starting over. However, living in a broken state isn't healthy for anyone. Living a life filled with peace and joy truly is one of the best sources of healing you can give to yourself when you make the decision to start over.

Key Questions to Ask:

- Do you have Peace?

- Do you have Joy?

- Are you holding on to things that you know that you should let go of, if so why?

- Why should you allow the opportunity for you to be healed?

- Are you afraid of the new changes of starting over, if so why?

- What does sacrifice mean to you?

- Is starting over hard for you and if so why?
  _____
  _____
  _____

- Do you feel broken, if so in what areas?
  _____
  _____
  _____

- Do you like being alone, if so why or why not?
  _____
  _____
  _____

- What do you want your fresh start to look like?
  _____
  _____
  _____

- What are some of the things that are hard for you to deal with?
  _____
  _____
  _____

- What are 3 things that is great about you?
  _____
  _____
  _____

- What is one thing that makes you who you are?

  _____
  _____
  _____

- What are 3 things that you want to work on or that you are going to work on?

  _____
  _____
  _____

Now you add some of your own questions or thoughts

Key Factors to Remember:

- Embrace Starting over and be the best you possible

- Don't be afraid of the change embrace it as though it was your first day of life

- Everything new will come with its own feelings don't contaminate it with the feelings of the old

- Peace and joy is one of the greatest strength to have, it says that no matter the storms you will hold on to your peace and joy because it will push you through the tough times

- Don't lose something that holds value

- Make the choice to be the person that thrives even after life has thrown you a curve ball

- After it is said and done, you have the power to raise above the testes and storms of life

- What you do with your opportunity is all up to you, if you do nothing then don't be mad at yourself or anyone else, just accept the lost if you are not going to be willing to put in the work

- There isn't a perfect person, but daily you can work towards the perfection of being your best person

- Every day will come with its own pros and cons it is up to you to keep your life balanced so that you can stay in harmony with your own personal peace and joy

- Focus on what matters and not on what doesn't

- Remember to always do a wellness check on yourself

How Do I Enjoy Life Being Single?

Enjoying life now that you are single comes with a mindset that says life is still great rather you are with someone or rather you are single. But of course you will miss the company of having someone and being able to do things with a partner and sharing intimacy if that was still something that was being shared; but that doesn't mean that you can't learn to do things on your own. If some of you were to be honest about when you were with your significate other, the two of you were only physically together where you shared the same space, but mentally you were checked out or they were checked out of the marriage or relationship. I say that to say for some of you, you may have felt like you were already single but still was holding on hoping things would change for the better.

I would like to encourage you by letting you know that there is life after a divorce or breakup and it can be wonderful. Life is what you make it, everything isn't always going to be great. Just like anything else you will find out that Relationships and Marriages will come with its own set of problems and challenges. So, how do you enjoy life being single? You have to now learn what it looks and feels like to care for yourself and what it looks like to learn how to do things by yourself, that part will take some getting use to, but it can be done.

You will also have to learn how to take care of the sole needs of yourself verses looking after the needs of another individual. You now have to learn how to make you the propriety. This can be challenging especially since you have been so use to seeing about the needs of someone else and having an attachment too someone else. You will first have to embrace that you are now single and not a couple. Next you will have to renew your mind while learning how to put your needs first and third you will have to transition yourself into spending time alone. As I stated before some of you were already living a single life or feeling as though you were single even though you were with someone. In this process you will learn to date yourself and get to know who you are again as an individual, which isn't a bad thing.

If you take the time to explore your singleness you will find out a lot about yourself. This is the beginning of how you learn to enjoy life being single. You have to take the necessary time to put you back together again so that you can first be healthy for yourself. Once these steps are taken and put in place, others may reap from your healthiness and they will also be able to share in your blissfulness. Spending time with yourself isn't as terrible as it may seem. Taking the time to reconnect back with yourself isn't bad; it will be well worth your wild. You will learn so many things about yourself, good and not so good in this process that will assist you in putting your life back together again.

Will loneliness come by to visit, but of course; do you have to entertain the loneliness, no you don't. Whatever you do, don't put all your focus on your singleness concentrate on your wholeness. Take care of your personal well-being and live each day working on yourself so that you can be your best person. It's not about being perfect or proving that you were the perfect catch. It is more so about you being healthy and whole; mind, body, spirit and soul. Believe it or not, it is in the dark and lonely places where we grow and get built up for the better and greater things that life has to offer. Just because you have experienced an unsuccessful marriage or relationship with someone, don't allow that failure to predict the rest of your life. For each failure learn from it, grow from it and build from it; but don't stay stuck in a dead place. Bury the past and all that has an attachment to it so that the new chapters can have a fresh start.

Key Questions to ask:

- Do you miss your ex-partner, if so why?

- Do you believe that you can be single and enjoy life?

- Do you feel as though you lost a part of you now that you are not with your ex?

- What does it feel like to be single?

- What do you miss about having a partner?

- What have you learned about yourself now that you are single?

- Can you name three things that was hard for you in your transition of being single?

  _____
  _____
  _____

- What was one thing that was easy for you to do when you transitioned into being single?

  _____
  _____
  _____

- If there was one thing that you would be willing to change about yoursef if anything, what would it be?

  _____
  _____
  _____

- What is your current level of joy on a scale from 1-5 with 5 being the highest?

  _____
  _____
  _____

- Have you learned how to enjoy life being single? If not have you taken the steps to learn?

  _____
  _____
  _____

- Have you gotten to the place where you would rather be single and not date anyone, if so how did you come to that decision?

  _____
  _____
  _____

- Are you open to marriage or dating again if you did the work of healing and you were equipped with the right tools and information?

  _____
  _____
  _____

- Do you feel free, if so what makes you feel free?

  _____
  _____
  _____

- Do you feel lost, if so why do you feel lost?

  _____
  _____
  _____

- Have you taken the time to Love You?

  _____
  _____
  _____

Now you add some of your own questions or thoughts

Key Factors to Remember:

- Enjoy life rather you are single or with someone

- Start the process of enjoying life and don't keep dwelling on the past but start living in your today

- No matter who was at fault point no fingers but use each day as an opportunity to become a stronger, healthier and purposeful you

- Remember it's ok to give yourself permission to start over, don't quit or give up

- Always remember there will be good days and not so good days but make the best out of each day

- Don't allow a failed marriage or relationship to define who you are or what you can have, remember you can have whatever you apply yourself to and whatever you put your mind to.

- Move, Move, Move, don't allow your feet to have no movement or negative movement, move one step and one day at a time. Remember that the present storm will and shall pass

- When no one is cheering for you always remember that you are your best cheerleader

- One day you will look back over the current place where you are now and you will be able to say, I made it, even though it was tough, it made me tougher

- Some storms, barriers or challenges will show you what you are made of whereas others will teach, train and prepare you for greater and better things or ventures

- Change your perception and views on how you see what did or didn't happen and be open to the true work that needs to take place within you

- It's easier to blame but it takes a person with a strong drive to say, I forgive you and not only do I forgive you, but; I forgive myself, be that person

How To Press Through Life Even When You Are Hurting

Everyone is going to face some kind of pain or sorrow that will leave them in a hurting or painful state. Don't dwell on the problem because it will only allow the hurt to continue to live in a place where it shouldn't be. Once you have identified the problem the next step is to find the solution. You can dwell on the pain or visit the pain or hurt, but don't live there; allow yourself the proper time to grieve. Staying in a painful or hurtful place shouldn't be an option, it should just be a pit stop along the way to your healing. You will have to press your way step by step, day by day. As you begin to take the necessary steps and time and put in the effort to be healed you will find yourself pressing through life even when it hurts.

It's when you do nothing and you allow yourself to soak in pity, you feel the pain and hurt lasting longer than you would if you actually took the time to do the work to be healed. I wish that I could tell you that you wasn't going to go through any pain or hurt, I mean I could; but I would be lying to you. Unfortunately, the hurt and the pain is a part of the process. How soon you come out of feeling the pain, hurt or distress will solely depend on you. I wish that life could sometimes stop or pause when we go through situations that require us to take a breather and push back from life where we can do nothing but take all the time we need to heal without having to take care of other things that needs our attention.

Unfortunately, that's not something that is always granted. When you press through anything in life it will require another level of strength that you didn't even know that you had. You will have to dig deeper because everything in you will say, I don't want to move, I just want to lay down and do nothing which sometimes can put you in a depressive state of mind. This is why it is important that you press through the pain and hurt so that you won't totally lose your drive to live and to be a healthier you. Remember the pressing is so that you can be in a better place working towards your best place mentally. Having an idle mind isn't good, you need to have your mind affixed on things that are good and that are positive.

Dwelling on the negative things will only hinder your process of healing. So you ask; how do you press through life when you are hurting? Don't allow yourself to feel overwhelmed, stay balanced and keep your mind as sharp as it can be considering what you are going through? Don't overdo it to the point that you experience burn-out. Only do things that are really important and mandatory. I know that sometimes we feel that everything is important, but when you have little to no energy you will find out fast what things are important and what will require your attention on a daily basis and what can wait.

You must remember that you are also in a place of restoration and being rebuilt so you don't have all that you had before this situation occurred. Some of you will find out that you only have a quarter of the energy that you once had while others may find out that you have half the energy that you once had and for some of you, you will find out that you don't have anything, your energy level is totally depleted.

There are a few things that is taking place at the same time during your pressing stage, which is the shedding of old things, and old stuff such as old thoughts, old ways, old behavior patterns, and an old mindset; along with your emotions being all over the place and so much more. Now on the flip side of that, there is also restoration and a rebuilding process that is taking place, this is the process where all of the old stuff is being removed off of you and being rebuilt so that the new things can grow and develop. So as you can see there is a lot going on at one time. When you are in the pressing stage, it is important that you press in moderation and stay balance because you owe nothing to no one at this point, but you.

Key Questions to ask:

- Have you started pressing through your hurt?

  _____
  _____
  _____

- Are you dwelling only on the pain and hurt or are you doing the necessary work that is needed?

  _____
  _____
  _____

- Where would you say that you are in the process of pressing through your hurt?

  _____
  _____
  _____

- How would you rate your energy level from 1-10 with 10 being the highest?

  _____
  _____
  _____

- Do you feel like you have something to prove to others, if so why?

  _____
  _____
  _____

- Are you staying balanced and are you not overloading yourself?

  _____
  _____
  _____

- Have you taken any time to heal yourself or do you think that nothing is wrong with you?

  _____
  _____
  _____

- What have you learned about yourself while pressing?

  _____
  _____
  _____

- Do you know how to identify a problem without staying there longer then you need to? If not what do you think you need to assist you along the way?

  _____
  _____
  _____

- Have you sat down with yourself to determine what things are important and what things can wait?

  _____
  _____
  _____

- Are you still functioning in the same manner as though you were still with your ex? If not what has changed?

  _____
  _____
  _____

- If so what hasn't changed?

  _____
  _____
  _____

- Rather you left your ex or your ex left you, do you believe that you are in a better place without them, despite the pain and hurt that you may feel?

  _____
  _____
  _____

- What is one of the biggest barriers or challenges that you face in this process of pressing through the hurt?

  _____
  _____
  _____

Now you add some of your own questions or thoughts

Key Factors to Remember:

- The pressing is for you and not for anyone else

- Everything starts with you and it ends with you, meaning this is your race and you run your race in balance, believing that you will arrive at the appropriate time

- Don't be quick to show the world or people the healed you before the process is done

- Timing is everything, with that being said remember to work on something that pertains to you everyday even if it is just taking in some quiet time

- Don't be so busy doing a lot of unproductive things that doesn't contribute to your overall healing and wholeness

- Remember to not only start the process of healing but to also finish to the end, don't do halfway because you deserve the whole 100%

- Remember to press until it doesn't hurt anymore

- There are many things that a person signs up for but not too many people sign up for self-care, be the one that knows the importance of self-care and give your mind and body a makeover

- Everyone goes through something in life no one is exempt. It's just that some people will have it a little harder than others. It doesn't mean that the other person life is better than yours, however, sometimes we can put more on ourselves then we can bare, then others times things happens that are out of our control; but either way, there isn't anything that you can't come back from if you apply yourself

- Give to your healing and it will give back to you in ways that will be fruitful to you

How To Get Back Up Once You Have Fallen

One of the key factors in life to remember when doing anything is to take one day at a time. You have to realize that there were things that lead up to the fall before the actually fall. Also, keep in mind it will take time to rebuild after any fall. It will also depend on your perception about the fall, meaning the divorce or the departure of the relationship. Everything that happens isn't all bad and even if it is; ask yourself, what good can you take away from it? One of the many things that I have learned along the way is; when people present themselves as pain and take you through unnecessary suffering, it is time for them to exit your life. Ask yourself this question, when did this person stop being an asset to your life or were they ever really an asset to your life?

The other question would be, were you the only asset in the relationship? In any marriage or relationship, it takes two to break or fix a situation or problem. If you don't take the necessary action when needed you will later learn that you are in the relationship or marriage by yourself. Oftentimes this is something that a person will realize once things have gotten way out of control. One of the many things that most are unaware of is; the power of agreement. This is one of the many factors that holds a relationship or marriage together along with both parties taking the time to learn how to dwell with one another. You will agree to disagree; you will disagree to agree.

Many people just jump right in and start living with someone without ever taking the time to learn them so that they can live with them accordingly. Some people will change; some for the better and others for the worst. Either way, ask yourself are you paying attention to the signs and are you having the conversations about any changes that you see that are effecting the marriage or relationship? See falls rarely just happen, there are some sort of sign or evidence that will appear before a fall. If you are not paying attention or you don't seek proper counsel to fix the problem, then expect a fall to come. If some of you were to be truthful with yourself, you saw things in your relationship or marriage that wasn't right before the divorce came or before the decision came to walk away. Problems just doesn't fix themselves, it takes the work and the willingness of the two parties who are involved in the marriage or relationship to fix what needs to be repaired.

Some people are good at playing the blame game instead of taking responsibility for what is theirs and fixing what is broken. So; how do you get back up after a fall? Start by working on yourself first. What I mean by this is, identify all that is broken within you and start the restoration process. Don't focus on the fall so much as the broken areas that needs to be repaired within you. It is easy to say what the other person faults were and never deal with the brokenness that lives within you.

One of the things that you need to ask yourself especially if you have been with someone for a long period of time and you felt or saw and knew things wasn't right, what kept you there? If you walked away but you kept jumping into relationships or marriages that had some of the same patterns, then why were you attractive to those types of people? Whatever the case might be, it's something that needs to be evaluated to make you better. No one wants to keep taking major falls in their life or falls at all for that matter. It's ok to sometimes trip but falls oftentimes require much more work.

Again focus on taking one day at a time, be honest with yourself without condemning yourself for having to be restored. Embrace your process and look forward to rebuilding your life. Don't allow life setbacks to predict the rest of your life. Don't put a cap on yourself or judge yourself harshly because you have had multiple marriages or many failed relationships, keep working on you until you become the best version of you. Be wiser about your choices.

Key Questions to ask:

- What have you learned from your fall?

  _____
  _____
  _____

- Have you ever taken the time to focus on you, if so for how long?

  _____
  _____
  _____

- What does a fall mean to you?

  _____
  _____
  _____

- Have you forgiven yourself for your part rather it be what you did do or didn't do in the marriage or relationship?

  _____
  _____
  _____

- Do you believe that you can learn and grow from this experience?

  _____
  _____
  _____

- What is your main focus?

  _____
  _____
  _____

- Have you set any goals if so what are two goals that you are going to achieve?

  _____
  _____
  _____

- How much time daily do you put into your self-healing?

  _____
  _____
  _____

- Out of all the questions that may run through your mind, what is the one question and answer that gives you peace of mind?

  _____
  _____
  _____

- Do you believe that all men are bad?

  _____
  _____
  _____

- Do you believe that all women are bad?

  _____
  _____
  _____

- How many times have you been married?

  _____
  _____
  _____

- Do you feel like you are a failure and if so why?

  _____
  _____
  _____

- How many unsuccessful relationships have you had?

  _____
  _____
  _____

- Do you judge your worth or value by the number of failed or unsuccessful marriages or relationships that you have had, if so why?

  _____
  _____
  _____

Now you add some of your own questions or thoughts

Key Factors to Remember:

- Remember that your life is what you make it, don't be afraid to start over when needed

- All falls aren't bad; you will be surprised what you learn in a fall

- Today is a new day don't get stuck on yesterday or your past

- We all will have storms, what matters the most is how you ride the wave until it calms and remember better days are on the way

- Do what works for you and what doesn't don't worry about it

- Don't allow life or situations to steal your smile and leave you with a frown

- When standing is all that you have left stand with peace and the belief that your life isn't always going to be like what you have experienced

- When others don't understand you, don't worry; keep pressing

- Refuse to allow condemnation to dominate your thoughts and actions

- Instead of beating yourself up, recognize your strength, power and ability to press your way through life

- There are levels to everything we do in life and when you go through the many different levels and stages of life remember that it isn't there to break you

- All that doesn't break you it will make you

- Don't be ashamed of your falls because we All have them; some people may experience public falls whereas others may have private falls, whichever way your fall is presented get back up and don't lie there

- Make the choice, that no matter the battle, test, storm or situation you will never give up on life, or being the best and the greatest expression of you

The Power Of One

You will learn that when you are alone some of your greatest dreams are birth. Being alone isn't always a bad thing. There is a difference in being alone and being lonely; most often people get the too mixed up. You can be alone and be perfectly content, it depends on where you are in your healing process and where you are in your life, meaning age, experiences and so forth. Don't talk yourself out of what you can have or do just because you are single. Remember this whole process is about the healing and restoration of you. This is a time for you to build yourself back up, also for some of you, it is a time for you to find yourself again. Take this time and invest in you and if you don't know how, then learn.

Oftentimes when a person is left to be by themselves they learn that they don't know what to do with themselves. When things don't work out for whatever the reason don't drown in pity or shame. If you do this for an extensive amount of time you will find yourself dwelling on the pain longer then you should be. You will later find yourself being held up in a place of grief and never getting anything done for yourself that is needed. It is ok to grieve because grievance is needed; but don't live there for years or longer then you have to.

When you were born it was only you and later in life you had dreams of what you wanted to do or what you wanted to be. Many of you with hopes that you will find a partner and you both can for fill life passions and dreams together. For some of you it may have started like that but for others you found yourself giving more to the marriage or relationship and you didn't get the things that you wanted or desired in life. I want you to take this time now that you are single to perfect the things that you wasn't able to work on while you were with your ex-partner. Take this time to work on the things in which your heart desires.

If you are older don't look at your age because there are many people your age and younger who still needs what you have to offer. Use this time while you are single to produce or reproduce the thing that you didn't get to do. Don't view yourself as poor old lonely me, see yourself as the One that will prosper rather you are by yourself or with someone. Your life shouldn't never stop because you are single. When a person comes to be in your life they should come to enhance your life, not take from it. You should be able to live your life as an individual and as a partner when you are with someone, this is something that seldom happens.

Most people pour so much of themselves into their partner to the point they lose who they are as an individual. They later find out that all of their dreams was placed on hold.

Truth be told that's another reason why some people become so bitter because they look at all that they had given up to get to the end of a thing to later realize all of what they really lost. For some of you, you may have been afforded to for fill a portion of your dreams, goals or vision with the partner you had but never to the full potential of what you could have had. Being alone gives you the time to focus and fine tune some things that needs to be done without the distractions or commitment that comes from being in a relationship or marriage.

I would like to encourage you that there is power in One, you just have to believe. Don't get so caught up in the power of two where you forget that there was a One before there was a two. The power lives within you. Always remember, anyone that is suppose to be with you or in your life wouldn't walked away. If you had to make the decision to walk away for whatever the reason was, trust yourself that you made the right and best decision for you. You shouldn't force something or someone to be in your life if it's not meant to be. What is meant to be will be and what is not, it won't.

Key Questions to ask:

- Do you know the power of One, if so what is it?

  _____
  _____
  _____

- Do you believe in you?

  _____
  _____
  _____

- Name one thing that you have learned from this chapter?

  _____
  _____
  _____

- Name one thing that is great about you?

  _____
  _____
  _____

- Name one thing that you are going to accomplish?

  _____
  _____
  _____

- What is a personal goal of yours that you placed on the back burner?

  _____
  _____
  _____

- Who are you as an individual person?

  _____
  _____
  _____

- What do you want out of life for yourself?

  _____
  _____
  _____

- Are you still grieving and if so how long has it been?

  _____
  _____
  _____

- Have you added up the cost of all that you didn't get done or wasn't able to get done when you were with your ex, if so what did you come up with?

  _____
  _____
  _____

- Did you gain more than you lost?

  _____
  _____
  _____

- Did you lose more than you gained?

  _____
  _____
  _____

- Did you lose and learn something and if so what was it?

  _____
  _____
  _____

Now you add some of your own questions or thoughts

Key Factors to Remember:

- Remember that anyone who is meant to be with you will remain in your life serving the purpose that they were meant for

- There are many things that one person can accomplish.

- Don't force things that shouldn't be

- Don't grieve longer then you should

- Remember that you were born with a purpose in mind so don't allow this one thing to stop your purpose in life

- People make mistakes, people change, people enter into relationships or marriages for different reasons other then what was agreed upon, nevertheless, don't stop being the light that you were created to be

- People are dysfunctional beings and sometimes you won't find out how dysfunctional a person really is until you marry them or you have a relationship with them

- Remember that sometimes a person will promise the moon and the stars but yet give you hell and bomb fires

- Don't ever let what you go through in life change who you are or take away who you were suppose to become

- If you fall get back up dust yourself off and start over

- Don't ever give so much of yourself to the point that you have nothing left for you, always keep a reserve

- Life will take you on all of these roller coaster rides, one thing that you need to remember is to hold on, brace yourself and whenever the ride stops pick up the things that are only needed for the next chapter of your life

Hope Deferred

In the book of Proverbs 13:12 amplified bible states: Hope deferred makes the heart sick, but when desire is fulfilled, it is a tree of life. For many of you this has been your experience. You have giving your ex-partner so many chances to get it right or to do the right thing which kept your heart in a deferred and sick state. You held on to hope wishing that he or she would change or do better but neither happen. They either got worse or they didn't care to change or fix whatever the problems or situation was so that you could have had a happy and healthier relationship or marriage.

Many of you have giving years and years of hoping, waiting and wishing for a positive change from your ex-partner but it didn't happen. This is why your heart is so heavy and burden. Hope deferred is just like anything else you are suppose to give it a beginning date and an end date especially when you are not seeing any progress or enough progress. What you will learn is that people will waste your time, while you are in a hope deferred place of waiting for change. Once you take an examination of the situation, you will learn that so much time had been given to the process but nothing had changed or the change that you did see wasn't anything to talk about or wasn't worth the wait.

Also, if there was some change it wasn't enough where it made the situation better where it wasn't no longer an issue. When people say that I have been like this all my life or this is how I am you can either take it or leave it, you should run and never look back. The reason why I say this is, if someone really wanted to change they would put forth the necessary time and effort daily towards change. Change starts with the renewing of your mind first, but if a person is going to keep the same mindset then you should expect the same behavior as well. Change is something that each individual will have to put in the effort and the proper amount of time and work in order to see real change.

One of the major problems in relationships and marriages are; people think that they can change the other person or people want you to do the work for them. It doesn't work like that each person has to do their own work towards positive growth and change. What usually happens is either one person is putting in the work and the other person is not or the other person is putting in very little work if any at all. Sometimes you will find out that no one is putting in the work because neither party believes that anything is wrong with them. Their belief is that there is something wrong with the other person because they are perfectly fine.

So now you either have two people saying I wish he would change or I wish she would change while in the meantime no real change is happening. Hope deferred makes the heart sick when no true change is taking place and it can be a waste of your time, energy, money and resources. One responsible thing to do is to take ownership of your own personal faults and imperfections and work on them. There will always be some work needed anytime there are two people who have made the choice to be together. Some people have had bad models which is one that I can attest to as it pertains to relationships or marriages. When you are in a hope deferred state; you should ask yourself, what are you giving hope to and what things really are going to be worked on? There is nothing wrong with having hope deferred but be reasonable about how much of your time that you are going to give. Don't give years to someone and you never see any real change. Don't let a person play with you to the point they show you a little change but yet they continue to do the same things as before and they say to you, they are working on it.

You will find yourself trapped in a Hope deferred place and half of your life will have passed you by. Be mindful of who and what you give your time to and don't cry over spilled milk because there is always a lesson in the mistake, you will just have to take the time to learn the lesson. Stay encouraged and keep your heart healthy. Never get stuck in a time capsule where nothing is moving but yet time and decades have past you by and you still are in a hope deferred place. Give a person an opportunity to change but never live in a place where you don't see true growth over a period of time. Of course use your best judgement, but don't spend decades and years allowing someone to mislead you and to make broken promises to you that hasn't shown results worth waiting on.

Key Questions to ask:

- What does hope deferred mean to you?
  _____
  _____
  _____

- What's in your heart?
  _____
  _____
  _____

- What are two things that you have learned from this chapter?
  _____
  _____
  _____

- How will you care for your heart so that it can be healthier?
  _____
  _____
  _____

- Did you give your ex-partner more time to change then needed, if so why?
  _____
  _____
  _____

- Did you believe that your relationship or marriage was going to work, if so why?

  _____
  _____
  _____

- When you were in the relationship or marriage what changes did you make if any?

  _____
  _____
  _____

- Did you find yourself always the one that was giving?

  _____
  _____
  _____

- What percentage would you say your ex-partner gave to the relationship or marriage?

  _____
  _____
  _____

- What was your expectations from your ex-partner?

  _____
  _____
  _____

- After reading this workbook would you say that you are ready to start your new beginning in a healthier state?

  _____
  _____
  _____

- Are you judging your mistakes or are you learning from them?

  _____
  _____
  _____

- Are you blaming your ex-partner or are you learning from the experience?

  _____
  _____
  _____

- Do you feel that you have been equipped with some information that you can use to assist you along your process?

  _____
  _____
  _____

- What are some of the things that you have learned about yourself?

  _____
  _____
  _____

- Are you now doing what you were born to do, if not are you heading down the path that will allow you to do so?

  _____
  _____
  _____

- Have you learned how to live a purpose filled life after the divorce or the relationship has ended?

  _____
  _____
  _____

Now you add some of your own questions or thoughts

Key Factors to Remember:

- Remember that hope deferred isn't a bad thing, you just don't want to give too much time to it where time and years pass you by and your heart grows sick and unhealthy

- Be mindful of how much of yourself that you are giving to someone

- Remember to Live your best life and don't get lost or caught up in the distractions

- Remember a relationship or marriage can be a blessing or a curse, if that person isn't the person for you

- Do the things that you never got the chance to do and become the person who you lost contact with, grow until you can't grow anymore, be all that you can be without the limits or restrictions

- Remember that you can have what you want but first you have to see it, believe it and then go after it, all is not lost, go for it

- Make the choice today that you will dig deeper inside of you to pull out all of the beautiful and wonderful things that have yet to be seen, you will first show them to yourself and then to the world because you are a person who is unstoppable and unbreakable

- No matter what damage has been done the repairs and the restoration along with the rebuild will shine shiner then the pain, hurt, shame or broken promises

- Don't ever stop believing in you even in the face of your enemies or adversity

- You have nothing to prove to others the work is for you but those who are watching you will reap from your healing and if not your life will minister to others your strength and your endurance to stand

How to live a purposeful life after the divorce or the relationship has ended?

Living a purposeful life will first start by you making the decision that your life still has purpose regardless of what you have been through. Sometimes when a person comes out of something that was traumatizing it can leave them with the impression that they have nothing to live for that holds any value because of a current situation. Oftentimes we base our future on a past or current event that we may be going through, which is never good. Living a purposeful life will start with you forgiving yourself and taking the necessary time and steps daily towards your healing. It will require for you to put in the effort to change and to fix what is broken within you. Also, you will need to renew your mindset and surround yourself around people or a person who is supportive, this could mean going to a support group. It will require for you to forgive yourself and the other person. It will also require for you to give yourself the opportunity to have a fresh and clean start. You will have to press into another level of strength in order to press through the pain, hurt, shame or humiliation.

You will need to give yourself permission to be restored and allow the proper realignment in every area of your life that needs it. Being bitter, upset or angry for long periods of time will only hinder your healing process. Nothing at this point really matters about the other person. Your fresh start has to start with you. The time framed to be healed will be different for everyone because everyone situation is slightly different even though it may look and sound the same. Remember to take baby steps until you are able to take bigger steps. Don't give up on you because there are new chapters in your life to write. The chapters are just waiting on you. I hope that this workbook has been a blessing to you and I wish you all the best on your journey of healing and starting over. Love other's, but Love You More!!!

www.ingramcontent.com/pod-product-compliance
Ingram Content Group UK Ltd.
Pitfield, Milton Keynes, MK11 3LW, UK
UKHW021326180426
11947UKWH00017B/1470